JOURNEY TO THE ALCARRIA

Camilo José Cela was born in Iria-Flavia, a tiny village in the province of La Coruña, Galicia, in 1916. His father was Spanish, his mother was English and one of his grandmothers Italian. He is recognized as a leader in the renaissance of the Spanish novel after the Civil War. His first novel, *The Family of Pascal Duarte* (1942), was an instant success and was followed by *Rest Home* and *The Hive*, the latter acclaimed as one of the best Spanish novels of the century, and probably the most spectacular. He was awarded the Nobel Prize for Literature in 1989.

Also by Camilo José Cela

The Family of Pascal Duarte

Mazurka for Two Dead Men

JOURNEY TO THE ALCARRIA

Camilo José Cela

TRANSLATED BY FRANCES M. LÓPEZ-MORILLAS

Granta Books
London

Granta Publications, 2/3 Hanover Yard, London N1 8BE

Originally published in Spain under the title *Viaje a la Alcarria*
First published in Great Britain by Granta Books 1990
This edition published by Granta Books 1998

A CIP catalogue record for this book is available
from the British Library.

3 5 7 9 10 8 6 4 2

Printed and bound in Great Britain
by Mackays of Chatham PLC

CONTENTS

To him who in the love of nature holds
Communion with her visible forms, she speaks
A various language.

WILLIAM CULLEN BRYANT

My dear Don Gregorio Marañón,

I am in your debt. There are many things about me which could not be explained without your generous and instructive friendship. I am not attempting to discharge my debt with these pages which I offer to you now. An inability to see things as they are is not, I believe, among my defects—especially when, as in this case, those things are as clear as electric light. I present this book to you with quite another intention. When debts are not paid because they cannot be paid, the best thing to do is not to talk about them, and shuffle the cards again. I am dedicating my *Journey to the Alcarria* to you because I know you are a lover of books about travels.

The Alcarria is a beautiful region which people apparently have no desire to visit. I walked through it for a number of days, and I liked it. It is a region of great variety, and except for honey (the dealers buy up all of that), it has everything: wheat, potatoes, goats, olives, tomatoes, and game. The people seemed like honest folk; they speak magnificent Spanish with a fine pure accent, and though they didn't know much about what I was doing there, they treated me well and fed me, sometimes scantily, but always with kindness. There was one town where they even made me a guest of honor of the town council and paid my bill at the inn; in another, perhaps by way of compensation, they threw me in jail by order of the mayor (who was a drunken, tongue-tied albino), and kept me there for a day and a night, locked in a stinking cellar and nourished on garlic soup and a couple of mouthfuls of wine dregs. There was a gypsy about my own age in the cell, who had stolen a mule. He thought, Heaven knows why, that I was a traveling actor, and kept asking me, "If you're an artist, why don't you say so?" The poor fellow simply couldn't get into his head that it wasn't because I didn't want to say so, but simply that I wasn't an artist. I don't mention this town in the book because I couldn't say much of anything pleasant about it.

When they turned me loose I kept on walking, and then, when I got tired, I came back to Madrid. In the Alcarria I went along writing down in a notebook everything I saw, and these notes were what I used as fodder for the book. I didn't see anything strange during my journey, nothing really shocking—a crime, or a triple birth, or a man possessed by devils, or anything of that sort—and I'm glad of it now, because since I had planned to tell exactly what I saw (for this book isn't a novel, it's more like a geography), if I start off telling horror stories people would say I was exaggerating and nobody would believe me. Anything goes in a novel, so long as it's told with common sense; but in geography, naturally, it's not the same, and one must always tell the truth because geography is like a science.

So, my dear Don Gregorio, that's all I wanted to tell you. It's little enough, but a stone gives less, as the saying goes. I'm sending you, too, a flower that I picked in a ditch; I've had it pressed inside a book all this time and now it's quite dried up. I think it's very pretty.

I beg you to accept this gift, offered with the best intentions in the world, by your devoted

C. J. C.

1. A FEW DAYS BEFORE

THE traveler is sprawled, face up, on a chaise longue covered in cretonne. He looks idly at the ceiling and lets his imagination wander freely; it flutters like a slow, dying butterfly, gently brushing the walls, the furniture, the lighted lamp. He is tired, and it gives him great comfort to let his legs fall, like marionettes, into the first position they happen to take.

The traveler is a young man, tall and thin. He is in shirt sleeves and is smoking a cigarette. For several hours now he has not spoken, for several hours he has had no one to talk to. Now and then he takes a swallow of whisky, or softly whistles a little tune.

All is silence in the house; the traveler's family is asleep. In the street only an occasional wandering taxi breaks in on the blessed isolation of the night watchmen.

The room is in a state of confusion. On the table, hundreds of disordered sheets of paper give evidence of many hours of work. Spread out on the floor, tacked up on the walls, are ten, twelve, fourteen maps with notes and jottings in ink, with heavy lines in red pencil, with little white flags stuck on with pins.

"Once I'm on the road, none of this is any good. That's the way it always happens!"

His jacket of heavy corduroy reposes on the back of a chair. On the rug, beside a pile of novels, rest his hobnailed walking boots. A new canteen awaits its burden of red wine. The last stroke of one of the small hours of the night sounds on the fine old walnut clock.

The traveler gets up, walks up and down the room, straightens a picture, smells some flowers. He stops before a map of the Iberian Peninsula, both hands in his trouser pockets, his brows almost imperceptibly drawn together.

The traveler speaks slowly, very slowly, to himself under his breath: "Yes, the Alcarria. It should be a good place for walking. And then we'll see; maybe I won't go out again; it depends."

The traveler lights another cigarette, serves himself another whisky.

"The Alcarria on the Guadalajara side; not the Cuenca side, not this time; towards Cuenca maybe I'll walk the pinewoods part."

The traveler makes a face. "And what difference does it make if I do go out of my way a little, if I go out of the way at all? After all, what does it matter?"

He turns over the papers on the table, looking for a ruler. He finds it, goes back to the wall again, and with his cigarette in his mouth and his brow knitted so that the smoke won't get in his eyes, he passes the ruler over the map.

"The day's walk to be neither long nor short, that's the secret. One league and an hour's rest, another league and another hour, and so on till the end. Twenty or twenty-five kilometers is a good day's march; it means spending the whole morning on the road. But then, once I get there, all this planning will be so much time wasted."

He looks up some notes, consults a little notebook, leafs through an old geography book, spreads out a map of the region on the table.

"Yes, of course I'll stick to natural regions. The rivers join and the mountains separate, that's the only real division."

The traveler's attention wanders for a moment and he takes out of the bookcase the first book his hand falls upon: the *History of Galicia* by Don Manuel Murguía. He has no need of it at all; to tell the truth, he picked it up without thinking.

"This is really amusing."

The traveler is half asleep and his head nods once or twice as he turns the pages. But he comes wide awake again when he reads the caption of a plate, "Cromlech located in Pontes de García Rodríguez." He returns the book to its place and reflects that really his books are rather badly arranged. The *History of Galicia* is between a *Physiology and Hygiene* of his high-school days and Hemingway's *The Sun Also Rises*.

The traveler goes back to the map.

"I'll go around the cities, like the peddlers and the gypsies."

He scratches one eyebrow and wrinkles his forehead. The traveler is not entirely convinced.

"No, I won't go around them. It's best to cross the cities in the late afternoon when all the girls come out to take a walk before Rosary."

The traveler smiles. His eyes are half closed, as though he were dreaming.

"Well, we'll see."

He is silent for a little while, thinking very confusedly, very rapidly. It is extremely late by now.

"Lord, what a mess!"

The traveler—who gets tired all at once, like a wounded bird—thinks at last that all he needs to do is to begin, that perhaps he is giving too much thought to a journey that he really wants to make a bit haphazardly, rather like a fire on a threshing floor.

He drinks the last swallow right out of the bottle.

"No, I'm anticipating, like the milkmaid in the fable. The best thing to do is grab my pack and start walking."

He gets undressed, unfolds the rough blanket, turns off the light, and lies down to sleep on the cretonne-covered chaise longue.

Outside, the distant thump of the night watchman's stick can be heard on the sidewalk. A little thread of light slips through the cracks in the blind. The first ragpickers' carts go by, slow and heavy-laden. The traveler has gone to sleep.

2. ON THE WAY TO GUADALAJARA

IT *WAS about the hour of dawn* . . . No, it wasn't even the hour of dawn; it was earlier than that.

The traveler (a few days later) gets up at the tag end, the blackest hour, of the night, even before the little gray birds of the city. He dresses by electric light in the midst of silence. He hasn't been up so early for years now. He feels an odd sensation, a sort of serenity, as though he had rediscovered something he ought not to have forgotten, as he shaves at this early hour when all the city's inhabitants are still asleep and its pulse, like an invalid's, beats quietly as if ashamed of being heard.

The traveler is cheerful. He whistles an approximation of a movie tune and then, shortly afterward, speaks to his wife, who has got up to cook his breakfast. The traveler is married. Married travelers, when they set off, always have someone to cook their breakfast at the last minute, someone to talk to while they shave in the wavering electric light that comes on in the early morning.

An hour before train time the traveler goes down the stairs of his house. He has just gone to take leave of his little boy, who is sleeping face down and warm, like a cub.

"Goodbye. Do you have everything?"

"Goodbye. Give me a kiss; yes, I think so."

The traveler, when he reaches the street, goes along singing quietly to himself. He has a poor ear and knows only the beginnings of songs. The subway is still closed and the slow, distant, rickety streetcars look like old donkeys—bulging, yellow, dead.

The traveler has his own philosophy of walking; he believes

that everything that comes along is always the best thing that could happen. It is best to go on foot, walking down the middle of the street, listening to the sound his nailed boots make as it rebounds off the houses. The windows of the houses are closed and the blinds are down. Behind the glass—who knows!—the men and women of the city are sleeping off their good or evil fortunes. There are houses that even look as though they shelter happy people, and whole streets that have a sinister stare, that seem to harbor men without a conscience, tradesmen, moneylenders, pimps, shifty bullies whose souls are spattered with blood. For all anyone knows, the houses of the fortunate people haven't so much as a sprig of mint or marjoram on the balcony. But sometimes the houses of people smothered by unhappiness, marked with the cruel brand of hate and desperation, are arrogant with balconies full of geraniums or overblown carnations as big as apples. The face that houses wear is a very mysterious thing; one could think about it for a long time.

The traveler, turning this over in his mind, goes along the walls of the Retiro and reaches the Puerta de Alcalá. He sees very clearly what he is thinking about, but what he is actually seeing is perhaps a little confused. Wary and diffident, the daylight struggles to reach the highest wires, the last rooftiles of the city, while the newly awakened sparrows chatter like mad things in the trees of the park. In the park, too, on the grass, is the republic of runaway cats, two dozen down-and-out cats with no masters, two dozen gray, wretched, mangy cats; they have no place beside a lighted hearth and they prowl in silence, like bored and hopeless prisoners or incurable invalids, forsaken by the hand of God.

The street doors of the houses are still closed, like stingy purses, and the night watchmen sporting shiny new gold braid on their caps look suspiciously at the traveler as he goes by on his way to the station with his knapsack on his back and his unworried, almost slouching walk.

The traveler is full of good intentions; he intends to lay open the heart of the wayfarer, to look into the souls of other travelers, peering into their eyes as one peers over the edge of a well. He has a good memory, and he wants to rid himself of every evil thought as he leaves the city, as if throwing out ballast. From his breast the verses of Don Antonio* come out audibly, rolling over the stones of the sidewalk—Don Antonio, the man with the dirtiest body and the cleanest soul who ever lived, as someone once said.

"When I come back, I'd like to be able to speak all those common truths that explain themselves as clearly as a river running. I'll be among honest folk who save for months, maybe even for years, to buy a little rug for the foot of the bed; and how I should like to be able to repeat, with kindly eyes and a look almost of resignation, Don Antonio's words of wisdom:

> 'Everywhere I have seen
> caravans of sadness,
> arrogant and melancholy
> drunkards with black shadows,
>
> 'and pedants standing in the wings
> who silently watch, and consider
> they are wise, for they don't drink
> of the wine of the taverns.
>
> 'Evil people who pass by
> and corrupt the ground they walk on . . .'"

Reciting his verses, the traveler reaches Cibeles Square. The last little bar girls of one of the nightclubs, in the first uncertain light of day, are selling a final dreary drink of anisette to the high-living young blades who are about to go home. The girls are young, very young; but they already seem to have in their eyes that special patient sorrow that one sees in hired animals, dragged hither and yon by bad luck and evil intentions.

The traveler goes off down the Paseo del Prado. Under the portico of the post office some urchins are sleeping in a dirty heap, all sprawled together on the hard stone. A woman passes by hurriedly, a square of lace on her head, on the way to early Mass, and a couple of policemen are sitting on a bench, smoking

*Antonio Machado, Spanish poet, 1875–1939. [Translator's note.]

languidly, with their carbines between their knees. The mysterious black streetcars of the night drag their scaffolding on wheels from one place to another; men without uniforms drive them, men wearing berets, silent as dead men, who cover their faces with scarves.

"I'd like to be able to tell the other part of the truth, too, for all things are to be found in the vineyard of the Lord:

'And everywhere I have seen
people who dance or play
whenever they can, and labor
in their little plot of ground.

'Never, if they come to a place,
do they ask where they have come.
When they travel, they go mounted
on the back of an old mule.

'They don't know the meaning of haste,
not even when there are feast-days.
When there is wine, they drink wine,
when there is no wine, cold water.

'They are simple folk who live
and labor, pass by and dream;
and one day, like so many others,
they rest underneath the earth.' "

Near the railings of the Botanical Garden the traveler feels—this happens to him sometimes—a sudden chill. He lights a cigarette and tries to drive the evil thoughts out of his head. Two streetcar men pass by with their hands in their pockets, cigarettes in their mouths, without saying a word. A ragged child is rooting with a stick in a mound of garbage. As the traveler goes by the child lifts his head and turns away abruptly, as if he wanted to hide. He does not know that appearances are deceptive, that many a rough exterior hides a heart of gold; that in the breast of this stranger, whose outside appearance is odd and even fearsome, he could find a heart as wide open as all outdoors. The child, looking as timid as a whipped dog, cannot know what infinite compassion the traveler feels for abandoned children, for wandering children who thrust a stick into the fresh, warm, aromatic heaps of garbage, just as dawn is breaking.

Some filthy, threadbare sheep pass by on their way to the slaughterhouse, with a B painted in red on their backs. The two men who are driving them hit them with their sticks from time to time, perhaps for sheer amusement; while they, with a look in their eyes half-wretched and half-stupid, doggedly lick the dirty barren asphalt as they go along.

A pretty little cart full of garden stuff comes rolling down the slope of Moyano Street. The secondhand-book stalls guard ever so closely their immense store of vain hopes that came to nothing, alas! without anyone's being the wiser.

On the street that slopes down to the station, various women offer the traveler tobacco, bananas, omelets between two chunks of bread. He sees soldiers with wooden suitcases on their shoulders and peasants in soft hats who are going back to their villages. In the gardens, among the chatter of thousands of sparrows, the whistle of a blackbird can be heard. The long, slow line for tickets is drawn up in the courtyard. A family is sleeping on an iron bench, under a sign that warns, "Beware of pickpockets." Advertisements of thirty-five years ago greet the traveler from the walls, remedies that no longer exist, porous plasters, underdrawers for the prevention of colds, the preposterous, sure-fire methods of combating baldness.

As he goes out to the platform, the traveler has a feeling almost of suffocation. The trains are sleeping in silence on the black rails, and the people go along in silence, too, as if frightened, trying to find a place to be comfortable among the rows of coaches. Some feeble light bulbs barely illuminate the scene. The traveler, while he looks for his third-class compartment, feels as though he were walking through an immense warehouse full of coffins, peopled with souls in torment bearing the double baggage of their sins and their works of charity.

The coach is in darkness. On the hard benches the travelers are smoking drowsily. From time to time one sees the tip of a cigarette glowing, or hears the scratch of a match which lights up for a few moments a reddish, unshaven face. Some workmen take seats, their jackets over their shoulders and their lunch-boxes, wrapped in handkerchiefs, on their knees. A group of fishermen come into the coach—wicker baskets slung on their backs—and carefully put down their long fishing poles. Women with big baskets on their arms come in; they are peasants who have come down to Madrid to sell eggs and sausage and cheese, to buy some printed cloth for a Sunday dress or a visored cap for their husbands. Two civil guardsmen settle themselves, one opposite the other, at one end of the compartment beside the door, under the emergency buzzer and the ceramic plaque that gives the section of the law pertaining to railroads.

The lights on the platform go out and now the darkness is absolute. At the last minute some cavalry soldiers scramble aboard; they are going to Alcalá de Henares and make the same journey every day.

The train starts; it is already seven o'clock. Suddenly, as the train emerges from the shed, the traveler discovers that it is fully light. Two trains are leaving at the same time and run parallel until the other one turns away toward Getafe. It is amusing to see them race along side by side while the passengers crowd to the windows to look at each other. Some wave and call out, as if encouraging the train to go faster. Inwardly—nobody knows why—the passengers on one train always envy slightly the passengers on another train; it is something that's true but a little difficult to explain. Maybe it's because, even though they don't realize it very clearly, a third-class passenger would always be glad to change places with another, even if the other were third-class too.

A startlingly rosy sky gleams over the city, glossy as a mirror, a sky that looks like colored glass. The train goes for a long time between sets of tracks and heaps of coal. There are worn-out engines, old retired locomotives, that look like horses killed in battle and put out to dry in the sun. In one uncoupled car standing by itself are crowded a dozen and a half black cows with long horns and meager hairy udders, who stoically await the hour of the butcher's dagger and the broad bleeding-knife. The traveler thinks that the animals must be dying of thirst, without knowing exactly what it is that is happening to them.

The sun appears over the horizon as the train crosses the last switch in the yards, the last signal, the last marker. At this hour there are no children playing in the outer suburbs. Far off to the south the Cerro de los Angeles stands all by itself. The fields are green and the crops well grown; it is hard to believe they are in the outskirts of Madrid. Between two cultivated fields is a fallow one, a field with poppies gently rippling in the light morning breeze. The train is already running clear along the track when the traveler turns away from the window, sits down, lights a cigarette and lays his head back.

As the train passes the stop at Vallecas, the silent atmosphere of the coach is violently shattered. A man in a lilac-colored jacket, with a handkerchief at his throat and a gold tooth, is offering at the top of his voice some strips of paper representing playing cards, each with a number on the back.

"Try your luck, ladies and gentlemen; a special package of fine candies or a bag of almonds, as you choose! Five céntimos a card! And then, in honor of my customers, I'll raffle off this Manolita doll, the sensational toy!"

The traveler decides to test his luck. He buys a strip and holds it in his hand a trifle doubtfully. The traveler is unpracticed in gambling. He lifts his head and looks out the window. Off toward the north, on the horizon, he can see the Sierra de Guadarrama with some of the peaks—La Maliciosa, Valdemartín, Las Cabezas de Hierro—still covered with snow.

The man with the gold tooth has given the usual spiel about honest hands and uncovered a card.

"The two of swords! Where's the two of swords? Who's the lucky one?"

The traveler didn't win; his few cents' worth was in face cards. The holder of the two of swords is a man who doesn't even smile. He takes the special package of fine candies without looking at anyone, almost scornfully, as if he wanted to give the impression that he is used to receiving important news without a flicker of emotion. Everybody looks at him, and possibly there is someone who admires him as well. What a way he has of carrying it off!

The traveler feels a sort of obligation to be a good fellow. He perceives something like a sudden flash of inspiration and raises his voice: "Give me all the threes; it's time the threes won."

Near Vicálvaro, the conductor goes through snipping tickets.

"That's the way to talk! This gentleman is going to take the prize for twenty céntimos! Here go the threes!"

The traveler half-closes his eyes and waits. He fully expects to hear, after a bit, "The three of—." The traveler intends to answer abruptly, "Stop right there; I have all four of them." Toward his right he can see some green hills with red clay cracks running down them. One of his fellow passengers is reading, with great attention, a weekly paper on bullfighting. A wasp is fluttering on the glass, up and then down. The voice of the man in the lilac-colored jacket resounds throughout the car.

"The seven of cups! Who has the seven of cups?"

The traveler trembles from head to foot, notices his heart beating violently, feels that his mouth is dry, squeezes his eyes shut. The traveler is afraid that all eyes are upon him, fastened like darts, smiling maliciously as if saying, "What happened to your threes?" The traveler begins to think, he doesn't know why—maybe to distract his attention—of river water flowing under a bridge. When he cautiously opens his eyes a little at a time he sees that no one is watching him.

The fishermen get off in San Fernando de Jarama. They sling their poles over their shoulders like rifles and set off, one after the other, along a path which leads to the river. On the other side of the river some fighting-bulls are grazing; they are black, solitary, silent, heavy, shining, replete with majesty.

The daylight is clear and transparent and the landscape shimmers like a postcard, with its green wheat and its red and yellow and blue flowers.

In Torrejón de Ardoz there is a station agent who uses sunglasses; he is a modern sort of chap. The name of the town, the station, and the sunglasses begin to resolve themselves into a little rhyme in the traveler's mind. He thinks for a while and then mutters to himself:

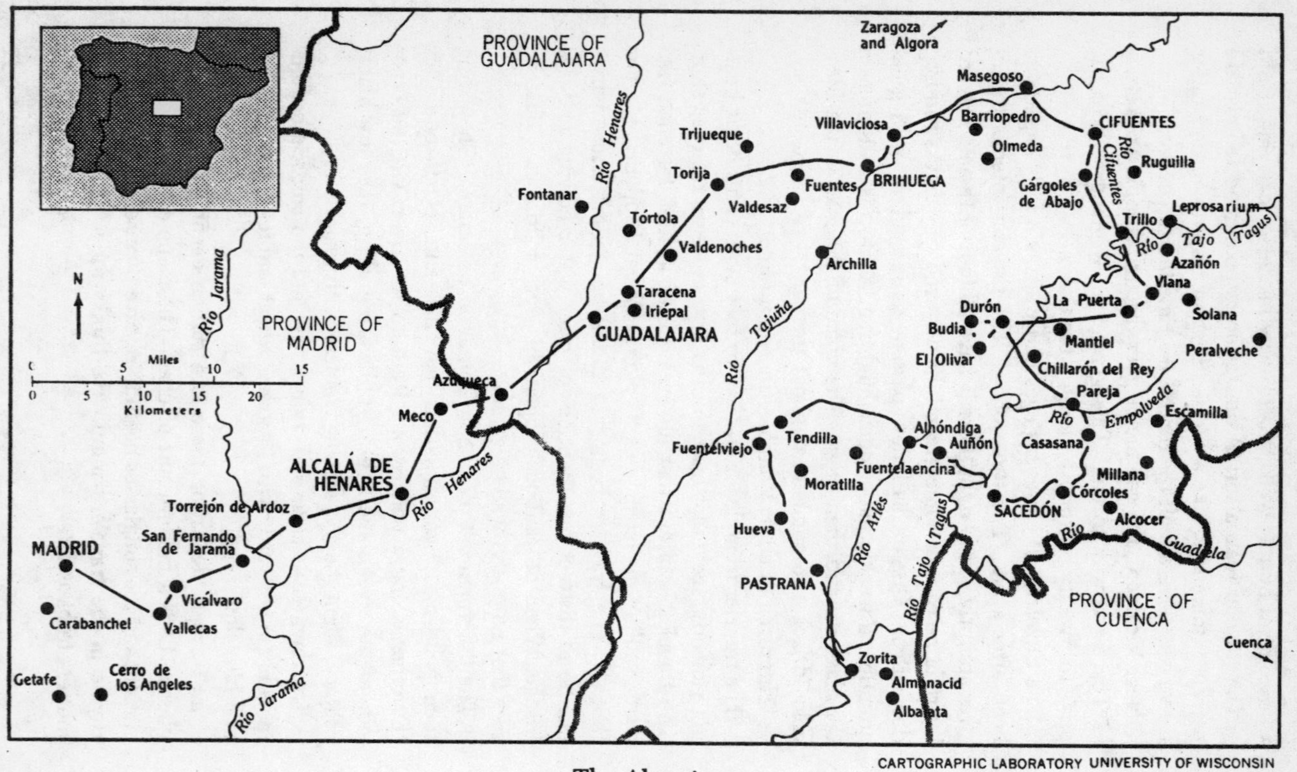

The Alcarria

CARTOGRAPHIC LABORATORY UNIVERSITY OF WISCONSIN

"The third-class coach is standing
Across from the W.C.
'Torrejón de Ardoz' is posted
In letters bold and free.

"With visored cap and glasses,
Well-shaded from the sun,
The agent walks the platform,
A minority of one."

The traveler laughs under his breath. Some workmen who look like Red Indians get on the train. Their faces are full of furrows, deep as knife scars, and their hair is black and plastered to their foreheads. A fat man who has the air of one of those traders who travel from fair to fair gets on too, smoking a cigar. It is seven-thirty in the morning. The traveler moves over to make a place for the man with the cigar.

"Thanks."

"Don't mention it."

The man takes off his hat and passes a handkerchief over his head.

"It's going to be hot."

"Yes, indeed."

"That is, unless we have a thunderstorm!"

The man breathes heavily as he settles himself in the seat. He takes the cigar out of his mouth and looks at it. His teeth are clay-colored and huge, like a donkey's.

"Yeah, that's what I say—if we don't wind up with a hailstorm!"

"Mmmm . . ."

The man takes out his packet of cigarette papers, pulls off two or three and sticks them to the cigar with saliva.

"There, it's better with a jacket."

"Obviously."

"Because without one it doesn't draw, y'know? These cigars are kinda tough."

The traveler's feet have been hurting him ever since he left Madrid. New boots will do that sometimes—they rub, and raise blisters. He digs around in his pack and produces another pair of boots, canvas ones with hemp soles.

"Looks like you're in trouble with your feet."

"Yes, some."

"That's to be expected; new boots."

"That's right; just as the proverb says."

The man with the cigar looks at the traveler. It seems he is going to ask, "What proverb?" But in the end he doesn't say anything.

Another man, smoking another cigar, comes along the corridor carrying a satchel. He looks as though he might be a medical orderly; he is a refined-looking young man who is wearing a striped shirt, salmon-color and white.

Near Alcalá de Henares the train goes past the walls of the cemetery. A little mist hangs, as always, over the river. In Alcalá de Henares a good many people get off, leaving the train almost empty: those fishermen who didn't leave the train at San Fernando, the cavalry soldiers, the men in black-visored caps, the great stout moustached women with the baskets. A blonde girl, who looks as if she should be called Raquel or Esperancita or some such name, with her hair done up in little curls held tight with spray and wearing a green-and-red-striped sweater, is flirting with a young civil guardsman whose moustache is cut "shaped," as the barbers says. The traveler reflects on love. The traveler has, in his house in Madrid, a French engraving called "L'amour et le Printemps." A bearded beggar goes down the platform picking up cigarette butts. His name is León and he is wearing sky-blue sandals. A man says to him, "Come here, León, you know how much I like you. Want a cigarette?" When León comes up to him, the man gives him a slap that cracks like the lash of a whip. Everybody laughs except León, who doesn't say a word; his eyes are full of tears, like a child's, and he goes off in silence, looking at the ground, bending over every little while to pick up a butt. At the other end of the platform León turns to look back. There is neither love nor hate in his eyes; they are like the eyes of a stuffed deer or an old disillusioned ox. He is bleeding from his nose.

In Meco, a milkman's cart is at the crossing, waiting for the train to go by. Some women dressed in mourning are carrying pails of water. The landscape is still green and flourishing. The traveler is eating apricots, taking them out of his pack.

"Have some?"

"No, thanks."

As a matter of fact, the man with the cigar doesn't look as if he would like apricots.

In Azuqueca, four mule drivers are plowing. The character with the cigar explains to the traveler that people from Azuqueca have the nickname of "brooders" because there's a yarn about how they put a broody hen to set on twelve eggs and no matter how hard they tried, they couldn't hatch out thirteen chicks.

The train runs along the banks of the Henares, close to Guadalajara now. Towards the end it goes fast, almost as if it were in a hurry.

Just before it gets to Guadalajara, the passengers collect their bundles and crowd onto the platforms and into the corridors. The traveler is the last to get off: what he is going to do can be done just as well a quarter of an hour later as sooner. Or he doesn't have to do it at all; nothing will happen.

The traveler slings his pack on his back, hangs his canteen from his belt buckle and starts walking up the hill toward the city. He crosses the river Henares, muddy and turbid at this point, and passes in front of a barracks. A few soldiers sitting in the doorway stare at him as he goes by. On his left as he climbs the hill, among the first houses of the city, the traveler sees a tavern with a beautiful name and goes in to have a drink. The tavern is called "The Best of the Grape."

The traveler deposits his impedimenta in a café near the place where the buses leave for the station, and goes to the telegraph office to send a telegram to his wife. The *Electrique Brillié* clock, hanging from gilded chains in the middle of the office, shows the hour of nine-thirty.

Back in the café the traveler buys some newspapers from a little boy who is quick as a mouse.

"How old are you?"

"Five and a half."

"What's your name?"

"Paco, to serve God and yourself."

"Sell a lot of papers?"

"Yes, señor; all of them. By twelve o'clock I've always sold them all. Last year, you know? I didn't used to. I was littler then and I couldn't run so fast!"

The traveler reads the papers while he has a second breakfast. Then he goes and takes a little turn around the town: he has to change some money at the bank. The palace of the Duke of Infantado is in ruins. It's a shame. It must have been a beautiful building, as large as a convent or a barracks. Down the middle of the street comes an idiot in a cap with a yellow visor, his face all covered with pimples. He is hurrying along, happy and optimistic. He is laughing like a loon, rubbing his hands together with pleasure; he is a happy idiot, a joyful idiot.

The traveler goes into one of those shops that sells absolutely everything.

"Do you have something typical of the town, something I could take as a souvenir of Guadalajara?"

"Something typical, you say?"

"Well, yes . . . that's what I said."

"I don't know. Unless you're thinking about Guadalajara tipsy-cake! . . ."

In a little harness shop that smells of leather and grease and has an owner so chubby and well-fed that he scarcely fits inside his shop, the traveler buys a leather headpiece.

"Is it for a mule?"

The traveler hesitates a moment.

"Yes indeed, for a mule; a Portuguese colt that's a real jewel. I want to dress him up in style. I'm going to give him to my wife's uncle who's a priest. In my part of the country the priests ride mules, see? Not like the ones around here who go on the buses. My wife's uncle's name is Rosendo and he's a canon. I named my colt Capitán; the other day somebody offered me double what I paid for him."

The traveler, as he finishes his speech, realizes that actually it hadn't been necessary to tell so many lies. The shopkeeper wasn't even listening.

"This is a good one; it's the best I have."

"Fine, that one then . . . Listen, do you mind putting the name of the shop and the date on the back? It's so my wife's uncle will know I'm not fooling, that I really bought it in Guadalajara."

"Yes, of course. Luisito! Luisito!"

From the murky back room comes a cracked childish voice. "I'm coming!"

"Listen, son, sign this, will you? It's for the gentleman here."

The boy looks at the traveler, takes pen and ink out of the drawer, and in the exquisitely careful calligraphy of the novice penman, writes on the back of the headpiece, on the untanned leather, "Casa Montes, Guadalajara, June 6, 1946."

3. FROM THE HENARES TO THE TAJUÑA

FROM Guadalajara, the traveler sets forth on foot by the main highway to Zaragoza, along the river. It is noontime and a fierce sunlight falls directly on the road. The traveler walks in the ditch, on the dirt; the asphalt is harsh and hot and hard on the feet. Going out of the city, the traveler passes a lunch bar which has a suggestive name, full of resonance, a bar called "The Mysteries of Tangiers." Just before this he had gone into a greengrocer's to buy some tomatoes.

"Can you give me three-quarters of a kilo of tomatoes?"

"Eh?"

The vegetable woman is deaf as a post.

"I said, can you give me three-quarters of a kilo of tomatoes?"

The woman doesn't move; she seems sunk in profound distrust.

"They're green."

"That's all right; they're to eat raw."

"Eh?"

"I said, I DON'T CARE!"

The woman considers, probably, that her duty lies in not selling green tomatoes.

"Are you going to Zaragoza for a vow?"

"No, señora."

"Eh?"

"I said, NO!"

"Because a lot of people used to go to Zaragoza; they used to carry their things on their backs, too."

"I'm sure they did, señora; now, can you give me three-quarters of a kilo of tomatoes?"

The traveler cannot shout any louder than he is shouting. His throat is dry; he would have paid five pesetas for a tomato. The door of the shop is full of children who are looking at the traveler; children of all sizes, with all colors of hair; children who don't talk or move, who stare fixedly like cats, without blinking.

A red-haired boy with his face covered with freckles tells the traveler, "She's deaf."

"So I can see, my boy."

The boy smiles.

"Are you going to Zaragoza for a vow?"

"No, my cherub; I am not going to Zaragoza. Do you know where I can buy three-quarters of a kilo of tomatoes?"

"Yes, señor; come with me."

The traveler, followed by twenty or twenty-five children, goes off in search of tomatoes. Some of the children run a few steps so they can get a good look at the traveler and keep up with him. Others get bored and drop behind. From the doorway of a house, a woman asks one of the children in a whisper, "What does he want?"

And the boy with the shock of red hair answers in a pleased tone, "Nothing; we're looking for tomatoes."

The woman isn't satisfied and makes another try.

"Is he going to Zaragoza?"

And the boy turns around and answers drily, almost indignantly, "No; do you think there's no place to go around here except Zaragoza?"

As he passes in front of the lunch bar, the man who—what a coincidence!—is not going to Zaragoza feels as though he has just been fished out of a pool where he was drowning. The traveler is with his helper; the boy with the saffron hair is beside him. The boy had said, "Will you permit me to accompany you for a few hectometers?"

And the traveler, who feels limitless admiration for children who speak pedantically, had told him, "Very well; I will permit you to accompany me for a few hectometers."

Now that he is on the highway, the traveler stops at a little stream to wash a bit. The water is cool and very clean.

"The water is very crystalline, isn't it?"

"Yes, my child; too crystalline for words."

The traveler takes off his pack and strips to the waist. The boy sits on a rock and watches him.

"You aren't very hairy."

"Well, . . . no; I suppose not."

The traveler squats down and begins to bathe his hands.

"Are you going very far?"

"Yeees . . . fairly far. Give me the soap."

The boy opens the soap dish and brings it to him. He is a very helpful boy.

"I was just thinking, if you're going very far in this heat—!"

"Sometimes it's even hotter. Give me the towel."

The boy gives him the towel.

"Were you born in Madrid?"

The traveler, while he dries himself, decides to take the offensive. "No, not in Madrid. What's your name?"

"Armando, at your service. Armando Mondéjar López."

"How old are you?"

"Thirteen."

"What are you studying for?"

"Technician."

"What kind of technician?"

"I don't know; just a technician."

"What does your father do?"

"He works in the provincial government."

"What's his name?"

"Pío."

"How many brothers and sisters do you have?"

"There are five of us; four boys and a girl. I'm the oldest."

"Are you all light-haired?"

"Yes, señor, all of us are red-haired; my father is too."

In the boy's voice there is a vague tone of sadness. The traveler wishes he hadn't asked so many questions. He thinks for a moment, as he puts away the towel and the soap and takes out the tomatoes, the bread, and a can of *foie gras*, that he has gone too far with his interrogation.

"Shall we have something to eat?"

"All right, if you want to."

The traveler tries to make himself agreeable, and little by little the boy begins to be happy again, as he was before he said, "Yes, all of us are red-haired; my father is too." The traveler tells the boy that he is not going to Zaragoza, that he is going to take a little trip through the Alcarria; he tells him where he was born, what his name is, how many brothers and sisters he has. By the time he tells him about a cousin of his who squints and lives in Málaga and is named Jenaro, the boy is helpless with laughter. Then he tells him about the war and the boy listens attentively, greatly impressed, with his eyes wide open.

"Did you ever get shot?"

The traveler and the boy have become great friends and they keep on, talking all the way, until they get to the road that goes to Iriépal. The boy says goodbye.

"I have to go back; my mother wants me to be home by lunchtime. And anyway she doesn't like to have me go this far—she's always telling me so."

The traveler puts out his hand, but the boy doesn't take it.

"It's because it's dirty, you know."

"Come on, don't be silly! What difference does that make?"

The boy looks at the ground.

"It's because I'm always putting my finger in my nose."

"What of it? I saw you do it. I stick my finger in my nose sometimes. It feels good, doesn't it?"

"Yes, señor; it does feel good."

The traveler starts off and the boy stays by the side of the road looking after him. When he has gone a long way the traveler turns around. The boy is waving goodbye. His hair shines like fire in the sunlight. The boy has beautiful, shining, enchanting hair, even though he believes the contrary.

A little farther on, the traveler sits down to eat in a gully, below an olive grove. Then he has a swallow of wine, unfolds his blanket and lies down to take a nap under a tree. Every now and then a bicycle or an official car goes down the highway.

Some distance away, sitting in the shade of an olive tree, a shepherd is singing. The sheep are huddled together motionless, half-dead with the heat. Lying on his blanket, the traveler has a close view of the life of insects as they dash from one place to another and then stop suddenly while they rhythmically wave their long, hair-thin antennae. The fields are green and well cared for, and the wild flowers—red poppies, white daisies, blue-flowered thistles, and the little golden buttons of the buttercups —grow along the edges of the highway outside the cultivated fields.

Some girls who have decorated their broad straw hats with sprigs of cornflower pass by; they are wearing flowered dresses and they walk freely, lightly, as graceful as gazelles. The traveler watches them go by and closes his eyes. He likes to fall asleep with the memory of some last pleasant sensation in his mind; a stork flying past, a child splashing in the backwater of a stream, a bee sucking the flowers on a thorn bush, a young woman walking in the first heat of summer with arms bare and hair loose on her shoulders.

The traveler, back on the road and fresh from his nap, thinks about things he hasn't thought of for many years, and he feels as though some little breeze had made his heart light.

When he gets to Taracena he fills his canteen with white wine. In Taracena there is no red wine—noble as the blood of animals, pungent and ancient as a terrifying family history. There is no inn in Taracena, either. No inn and no lodging of any kind. But there is a cool, clean tavern in Taracena with a freshly sprinkled earthen floor. The woman who keeps the tavern has a very studious little girl; a girl of ten who gets up from her nap without being told and goes back to school.

Taracena is a town of adobe houses, an ashy, light-gray town; a town that seems to be covered with a dust as fine and delicate as the dust on books which have rested for years on the shelf without being touched or disturbed. The traveler recalls Taracena as being uninhabited. He doesn't see a soul. In the heat of four o'clock in the afternoon, there is only a child playing apathetically with some apricot pits. A mule cart, with its long tongue lying on the ground, is baking in the middle of a little plaza. A few hens are scratching in some heaps of dung. On the front of a house, some well-washed shirts, so stiff and rigid that they seem to be made of cardboard, shine like snow.

The traveler chats with the woman of the tavern.

"Is there water in the town, señora?"

"Yes, señor, a great deal of water, and very good, too. We have the same water here as in the capital."

The traveler sets off again; since it is the first day, his legs are a little tired. The woman comes to the door to say goodbye to him.

"Goodbye, and good luck. Are you going to Zaragoza?"

"Goodbye, señora, many thanks. No, I'm not going to Zaragoza."

The traveler reflects on the farewells given to men who travel, a little like the farewell one gives to those one will never see again. The "Goodbye, and good luck" that the country girl or the tavern woman or the washerwoman or the mule driver gives, is a farewell forever, a lifelong farewell, a farewell laden with unrecognized sorrow. Their souls and all their five senses go into that "Goodbye, and good luck."

A bare half-league farther on, where the road branches off to Tórtola and Fontanar, the traveler catches up with a cart. The traveler discovered later—in Cifuentes, a place where he learned a great many things—that in the Alcarria they call the people from Tórtola "Moors," and the people from Fontanar "Stalkers" because once they used a stalk of wild cabbage to serve as an eye for the image of Saint Matthias, who is the patron saint of the village. The cart driver is asleep and every now and then the mules let the wheels go over the piles of gravel at the side of the road. Then the driver wakes up, swears, straightens out the cart, and goes back to sleep.

"Good afternoon."

"And a hot one, too."

"You look pretty comfortable."

"Not bad. Would you like a ride?"

"Well, if you insist!"

The driver stops his mules and the traveler jumps in. The cart has a low canvas awning which produces a suffocating heat. The traveler invites the driver to have a swig from his canteen.

"Good wine."

"It's not bad; I bought it down in Taracena."

Then they have a cigarette. The flame of the lighter doesn't even waver.

There are some wooden doors and an iron bedstead in the cart. The traveler cannot even change his position; his legs are doubled up and his head leaning back, with his pack serving as a pillow.

"How far are you going?"

"To Trijueque; in the mornings I go down to Guadalajara with firewood. You going far?"

"No, I'm staying in Torija; I plan to spend the night there."

"And tomorrow?"

"Tomorrow, God will dispose."

The driver reflects for a moment.

"Well, if you're going on foot you have a good long walk ahead!"

"I suppose so."

The driver is a young man, short and weatherbeaten. His name is Martín Díaz and he is a native of Trijueque. When he gets a little friendlier he invites the traveler to have some bread and onions.

"This is good for the blood."

An old man comes down the road from the opposite direction and passes by; he is riding a speckled mule with delicate legs and a tight croup. The man has his head and shoulders covered with a blanket.

"Good mule!"

"So it seems."

Martín Díaz is a stoical and optimistic cart driver, a driver who finds good in everything. Going from Trijueque to Guadalajara and back again, Martín Díaz has learned to see the good side of things.

"These two mules of mine are kind of worked-out, but they

can still do their stuff."

Martín looks at his mules.

"I bought them cheap. They've gone up a lot now; these days a mule costs a fortune."

The traveler watches the mules walking, their harness taut as they go uphill, loose and as if resting on the downslope. The mules move their ears in rhythm as they go, making the little bronze bells on the horse leather tinkle. Martín calls the collar a horse leather.

"This one's name is Catalana; the lead mule is called Pantalón."

Near Valdenoches some laborers are breaking stone. They are black as soot and wear handkerchiefs under their caps to soak up the sweat. They work slowly and wearily, and protect their eyes with a little piece of wire screen tied at the nape of the neck with strings. When the cart goes by they do not raise their heads.

After passing the hills of Sotorija and El Tío Negro, the cart goes along a broad road with elms on either side.

"You can breathe here, can't you?"

"I should say so."

"Well, from here on to Torija the road is just like this."

Well-tended garden plots begin to appear at the right of the road. The old men are in shirt sleeves with the top button fastened, and corduroy trousers with a sash around the waist. Some of the young men wear coveralls of blue cloth.

Just at the edge of Torija some women are singing as they wash clothes. As they see the cart pass they stop their work for a moment and call a cheerful greeting, smiling.

The town of Torija is built on a hill. As one comes into it from this direction, it looks very noble with its castle and its square-towered church. On the wall of a house there is a sign which reads, "To Algora, 39 kilometers. To Zaragoza, 248." It is a blue sign with big white letters, one which could be seen perfectly clearly even by someone who went by very fast in an automobile.

In Torija the traveler gets down from the cart in front of the inn, on the far side of the town. Before this he has had a glass of wine with Martín and has talked with him about the weather, about how well the wheat has grown, about what a pair of mules is worth, about how long a corduroy jacket will last, about how stuck-up the maids in Madrid are (they're nobody, they're just like any other girls, but with the airs and graces they put on, you'd think they were countesses). The driver and the traveler agree that the best thing to do is not even to look at them and to marry a village girl, the kind of girl a man knows all about and has some idea of what she's been up to.

"The ones that go to Madrid, a man doesn't know a thing about. Maybe they come back the way God made them and then again maybe they come back as sassy as so many chorus girls!"

The traveler, seated on a stone bench at the door of the inn, watches Martín Díaz go off along the road to Trijueque. The driver has taken off the little canvas awning and is urging his mules along. They go faster now that they sense their stable.

Before they go around the bend in the highway the traveler takes a last look at the cart, at Martín Díaz, at Catalana and Pantalón, who will go down to Guadalajara again very early tomorrow morning with their load of wood.

The traveler washes up in the entrance way, in a basin placed on a rush-seated chair. A child is crying halfheartedly. The chickens are beginning to roost. A filthy dog sniffs around the traveler's feet. The traveler gives him a kick and the dog retreats with his tail between his legs. One can see that he is used to receiving kicks. A little girl is playing with a black-and-white cat. A donkey passes, all alone, on his way to the stable; he pushes open the door with his muzzle and slips inside.

The traveler talks with the woman at the inn.

"What's the name of this inn?"

"It doesn't have a name. My mother is called Marcelina García."

The traveler keeps trying.

"You have a fine castle here!"

The woman looks the traveler in the eye.

"Yes, it's very old. People say it's been there since the time of the Moors."

A young man goes by with a dark-colored mule.

"Eh, Generosa! Giddap, Generosa!"

The daughter of Marcelina García talks with the traveler.

"Will you be having wine?"

"Yes."

The woman raises her voice: "Niña, go get some wine!"

The little girl goes to the kitchen and comes out with an empty bottle in her hand. The inn in Torija is an inn where there is no wine, an inn where the child has to go and get it when they ask a traveler, "Will you be having wine?" and he says that he will.

"Do you want red or white?"

"Red."

The traveler goes into the dining room to fix up his pack a little.

The table is covered in oilcloth with a pattern of pink and white diamonds. The sideboard goes up to the ceiling. On the wall there is a relief map of the Iberian Peninsula and a colored lithograph of Pears's "Christmas Gift." A wall clock with a mother-of-pearl face indicates the supper hour. Hanging from the ceiling around the light bulb are four round tin cans, the kind pickled fish come in. There is a twining plant growing in the cans, forming garlands; its name is "Love of Man." The bulb is unlit.

"What about the electricity?"

"It comes on later."

The traveler eats his supper by the light of an oil lamp. Beans with sausage, a potato omelet with onions, and goat's meat which is hard as a rock. For dessert he has a glass of goat's milk.

When the electricity does come on, well after dark, the filament in the bulb only reddens slightly, like a live coal. Seen through the hanging ivy, the lighted bulb looks like a firefly.

"When the light really comes on full strength just before morning, it shines like the sun, you'll see."

The woman of the inn smiles when she talks. She is a pleasant woman and full of good intentions. The traveler goes up to his bedroom. There is a large, handsome iron bed with a thick straw mattress. The traveler turns the light switch to "on" and undresses in the dark. When the light does come on full strength, shortly before dawn, it sheds an opaque light over the room, a light that would just serve to develop film but by which it would be difficult to read.

A young man is singing at the top of his voice; he makes a tremendous amount of noise, and can surely be heard a long way off.

> "If you're looking for a sweetheart in Teruel,
> Be sure she's a stranger to the town;
> For the women who come from there
> Will kill a man with love."

As she serves his breakfast, the woman of the inn tells the traveler, "That fellow you heard singing early this morning is my brother. He sings in the Aragonese style. When he was a soldier he was in Zaragoza, and that's where he learned to sing that way. He has a good voice, hasn't he?"

"He certainly has!"

It is still very early when the traveler takes to the road again. It is rather a cool morning and the sky is somewhat clouded over. A little later, when the sun begins to beat down, the clouds will disappear and the air will begin to warm up. A short way along the road the land begins to be slightly hilly. To the north one can see Trijueque, from which Martín Díaz has no doubt set out already with his mules. There is not a single tree to be seen. A man passes, riding on a huge mule.

"Good day to you."

"May God send us many more. Are you going to Brihuega?"

"Yes, señor; that's where I'm going."

"You have a good long way to go. If I had a different mule I'd take your pack at least."

"Many thanks, but it can't be helped. I'm still fairly fresh."

"You'd be better off with me. But I don't dare put you on this one. She's a sort of mongrel mule and pretty unreliable. When she gets fed up and takes a notion to be ornery, she starts to kick and nobody can manage her. I hit her and hit her, but she doesn't pay a speck of attention!"

The traveler keeps on following the road, his pack on his back. After every hour, every league of walking, he sits down in the ditch to have a swig of wine, smoke a cigarette, and rest a while.

In the fields he can see peasants plowing the ground with their teams of mules. Some twenty paces away from the traveler a flock of doves rises in flight. Two buses jammed with people pass by in a cloud of dust, one directly behind the other.

A good league on from Torija the oaks begin to appear, scattered at first and then in clumps. A shepherd walks unhurriedly after his sheep, along the side of a hill. The only sound to be heard is the chirping of the swallows and the song of the larks. A little later the houses of Fuentes come into view, with the church tower in the midst of them.

Fuentes de la Alcarria is at the right of the road. The little oak wood has become thicker. The countryside has a strong deep smell, and bees are sucking in the thorn bushes with their masses of tiny white flowers. Two rabbits, crouched back with their ears twitching, stare at the traveler for an instant and then run away quickly to hide behind some rocks. An eagle is flying in circles overhead, not far away. A woman riding on a donkey meets and passes the traveler. He speaks to her, and the woman neither looks at him nor answers. She is a young woman, pale and beautiful, dressed in mourning, with a kerchief on her head and with great deep dark eyes. The traveler turns around. The woman is absolutely motionless, letting the pace of the strong, sturdy donkey carry her along. One would think she was a dead woman without mourners, going alone to the cemetery to be buried.

The traveler takes an extra swallow of wine for comfort, and goes to sit at the foot of a tree near the walls of the palace of Ibarra, which is beside the highway. The palace of Ibarra is a huge place half in ruins, with an abandoned garden which is full of enchantment; it is like an exhausted dancer, gentle and ill, breathing the health-giving air of the countryfolk. The garden is choked with undergrowth. A goat tied with a rope is dozing and chewing, stretched out in the sun, and a hairy little donkey is frisking about, kicking at the air like a mad creature. A tall, slim Japanese pine rises out of the brambles; it has a graceful and aristocratic air and seems like an old ruined nobleman, formerly proud but today the debtor of those who used to serve him.

A league farther on, the wood comes to an end and there is

cultivated land again. A few puddles are visible in the fields. An old man complains to the traveler.

"Don't you believe that's a good thing. It's rained too much. The Alcarria needs its water, you know, but not too much and not too little."

The traveler thinks to himself that a man who talks like that runs the risk of always being right.

Now the highway describes a great curve, and after passing a crossroads the traveler suddenly finds himself in view of Brihuega, which is in a hollow. Two highways branch off from the crossroads in addition to the one the traveler is walking on—a left-hand one which goes to Utande and a right-hand one going to Álgora, back on the main highway.

To get down to Brihuega there is a shortcut which saves considerable time. The traveler sets off along the shortcut, which is full of stones and appears to be the dry bed of a seasonal stream. A little more than halfway along it he meets a shepherd boy sitting on a stone beside a broken wall, a wall which no longer encloses anything.

"Niño, what's the name of this gully?"

The boy doesn't answer.

"Listen, I'm talking to you. I said, what's the name of this gully?"

The boy is all confused and doesn't know what to do with himself. He looks at the traveler's feet, blushes up to his ears, and strokes his knee. At last he finds the courage to answer in a thin little voice, "It doesn't have any name."

The traveler gives the boy a few coins, which he didn't want to accept at first.

From the path Brihuega has a very fine appearance, with its walls and its old cloth-factory as big and round as a bullring. Behind the town flows the river Tajuña, with its leafy banks and its green meadows.

Brihuega has a bluish-gray color almost like that of cigar smoke. It has the look of an old city, with a great many stone buildings, well-constructed houses, and big stout trees. The scenery has changed all of a sudden, as though someone had thrown back a curtain.

4. BRIHUEGA

THE one who did know the name of the shortcut, though, was a man with a stutter who, in the shade of an ancient elm beside the inn called Las Eras, was preparing onion sprouts for planting. When the traveler asks him about it the stuttering man laughs.

"It has a very dirty name, see?"

The traveler gives him a cigarette.

"But not one that can't be mentioned, I should think."

"Oh, yes, it can be mentioned all right."

The man has a great deal of trouble talking. Between the stutter and the laughter he is barely understandable.

"Almost in the middle of the path there's a fountain we call the Fountain of Quiñoneros."

"And the shortcut has the same name?"

"No, señor; that's not its name."

The man is convulsed with laughter. A woman with a child dangling from her breast says to him, "Go on, you're acting like a fool! He wants to know, doesn't he? Well, tell him!"

The woman probably feels like saying, "The devil take him with all those questions he asks!"

But she didn't say so; undoubtedly she thought it. The stuttering man puts his head to one side and makes up his mind.

"Well, the shortcut is named, anyway that's what we call it, the path to Shit Fountain."

The traveler thinks that the man of the onion sprouts is a very delicate-minded stutterer; there wasn't so much to make a fuss about. When the traveler moves away, the stutterer is still laughing to himself as he cuts with a tremendous butcher knife the tender sprouts he is going to plant that afternoon.

The traveler goes into the inn to eat. But beforehand he gives himself a footbath, a hot bath with salt that makes a new man of him. A provincial young lady and her mother are in the dining room.

"Good day to you; may you enjoy your meal."

"And to you too. Many thanks."

The girl drinks white wine and takes calcium tablets. She is a pale creature with well-shaped hands and chestnut hair combed into little curls that fall over her forehead. From time to time she coughs delicately.

On the walls of the dining room are a clock with weights, a canary named Mauricio in a cage of gilded wire, and three reproductions in violent, screaming colors with metal frames. One of the pictures is Velázquez's "The Surrender of Breda," another is his "The Drunkards," and the other Murillo's "Holy Family with Bird." Two cats are prowling about to see what they can find to eat. One is light-colored and is called Blondie, the other is dark and is called Brownie. There's no doubt that the person who named them displayed real imagination.

The traveler is served by an attractive, somewhat flirtatious girl, who is wearing a percale dress.

"What's your name?"

"Merceditas, at your service. I'm called Merche."

"It's a very pretty name."

"No, señor, it's a very ugly name."

"How old are you?"

"Seventeen."

"You're very young——"

"No, señor; I'm not so very young any more."

"Do you have a sweetheart?"

"Ooh, you want to know a lot!"

The girl turns pink and rushes off to the kitchen. When she comes back she is very serious and changes the traveler's plate without looking at him.

"What's the matter?"

"Nothing."

A clumsy countrified maid is helping Merche; the traveler doesn't find out what her name is. The oilcloth on the table is yellow, with the color worn off in places and the edges somewhat raveled. A "girlie" calendar on the wall advertises anisette. The girl is a blonde with black eyes, wearing a green dress that leaves her shoulders bare. She has her hair in a low knot and wears a very shiny comb which is immediately noticeable, a comb made of that silver dust they use for stars in a Christmas crèche. At the window of the dining room there is an iron grille, the kind you see on balconies, placed sideways.

When he has finished eating, the traveler goes out on the street. He had thought about resting for a while after his coffee, but two gentlemen who came into the dining room made him nervous and he decided to get up and go.

Beside the inn the traveler finds the Puerta de la Cadena, the gate through which one enters the town. The Puerta de la Cadena has a niche with a statue of the Virgin in it, and a white marble plaque underneath, reading, "1710–1910. The town of Brihuega on the two hundredth anniversary of its memorable bombardment and attack," and still lower down another plaque of stone which is only partly legible.

The plaque looked more or less like this: *

PORESTA PVERTASDE LA B ZE N
YASALTO E L D 9 DE DE BRD 1710. POR
LASARMAS D SV MAG NR OR
PHE L PE V CON TRA A STRO PAS Y N L B G S A S
IOL DSA S. QEST VAPOD TA P ZA AB D V S
R L PERSONA

*Through this gate on December 9, 1710, the troops of His Majesty Our King Philip V advanced to the assault against the English and Dutch troops who were in possession of it, led by His Majesty in person. [Translator's note.]

The traveler copies down the letters on a piece of paper. It takes him some time, for he makes a mistake occasionally. People crowd around him. The traveler is immensely pleased that they take him for a scholar.

It's not very well copied, to be sure; but not a single letter is missing and that's the truth. Almost all of it is fairly clear, but there is a bit at the end which isn't, at least to the traveler. In the next-to-last line, toward the middle between the T and the V, there is a hole which must have been made by grapeshot.

The traveler goes in, as has been said, by the Puerta de la Cadena, and wanders about the town for a while. On the other side of the Puerta there is a charming, shady grove of poplars. Some girls are chatting on a bench. They are laughing at the tops of their voices and slapping their thighs. Then they get up and go to drink water at the fountain.

Inside the city wall some shearers are clipping sheep in a stable open to the street. The wool comes off whole like an undergarment, heavy with grease, and the sheep are left naked and skinny, with their bellies swollen and an ungainly look about them. Some boys are watching with unhealthy interest while they smile in silence. To watch sheep being sheared in a stable which is more than warm, which is oppressively hot and has a sour reek to it, is a soporific sight, a sort of atavistic excitement that tends to stir up young boys who, without stopping to think why, confuse sexual appetite and cruelty in an ancient and unconfessable tumult of the blood.

The sun is halfway down in the sky. For a moment all women look beautiful to the traveler. He sits down on a stone, his heart suddenly heavy, and watches a group of eight or ten girls who are washing clothes. The traveler is deep in thought and somewhat abstracted, and soft pagan wisps of cloud fill his memory as he recalls the ever-fresh lines of the medieval song:

Mother, see, the maidens,
  The maidens of the town,
Are washing in the river;
Their shifts they wash with water,
  The water running down.

The girls have their sleeves rolled up. One of them is singing a snatch of operetta, another an out-of-date popular song of four or five years past. A girl who isn't singing has some blue flowers in her hair. She can't be seen clearly but from the back she looks like Merche, the girl at the inn.

"My name is very ugly . . . I'm not so very young any more . . ."

The next day, when the traveler is already on the road, he thinks of the days that are no more; he closes his eyes for a moment to feel the beat of his heart.

An old light-colored ox with long horns and a sharp thin face like a knight of Toledo is drinking from the basin of a brimming fountain beside the washing place, barely dipping his grizzled muzzle into the water. When he has finished drinking he lifts his head and passes behind the women, humble and wise. He seems like a loyal eunuch, bored and discreet, who guards a harem as turbulent as the break of day. The traveler follows the animal's slow, resigned progress with perplexed eyes. Sometimes the traveler feels completely transfixed by things he cannot possibly explain.

Two dogs are making love violently, obstinately and shamelessly out in the sun. A setting hen goes by, surrounded by chicks as yellow as grain. A goat looks out of a side street with his head up, his eyes fathomless, his horns proud and threatening. The traveler looks for the last time toward the girls who are washing, gets up and goes away. The traveler is a man whose life is crisscrossed with renunciations.

The traveler walks down a few narrow streets and smokes a cigarette with an old man at the door of a house.

"This seems like a fine town."

"It's not bad. But you should have seen it before the war, when the airplanes came."

The people of Brihuega talk about before and after the airplanes the way Christians talk about before and after the Flood.

"Now it's not even a shadow of what it was before."

The old man feels contemplative and mournful. The traveler looks down at the pebbles on the street and lets his words fall slowly and almost at random.

"Good-looking girls too, from what I've seen."

"Bah! Don't even look at them; they're not worth a damn. If you'd known their mothers!"

The old man, whose head is very shaky, sighs and changes the subject.

"This is where the Italians turned tail and ran, did you know that?"

"Yes, I know."

"That was really good!"

The old man gets up and goes into the house. A little later he comes out again, leaning heavily on his cane.

"You'll excuse me; I went to look at a pot on the stove."

The old man sits down again and rests his cheek on his hand.

"At my age a man's no good for anything, all we old fellows can do is watch pots. I'm an old ruin now, but you should have seen me when I was young!"

The traveler muses that what has happened to the old man is what has happened to Brihuega—you should have seen it before! —and that this is what happens to everyone and everything. The traveler, who would rather not feel depressed today, gets up and takes his leave of the old man and then heads on down the hill. He passes some arcades—wooden beams for columns with a square stone for a base—and arrives at a little shop so varied, crammed with so many things, so picturesque, that it seems to have been put there by the Tourist Department.

The owner is a crafty man, squint-eyed, portly and thoroughly nasty, who knows exactly where every shoe pinches. He talks about everything and anything, and gives himself airs of being a poet and a man of culture.

"Welcome to Casa Portillo!"

"Thanks."

"Casa Portillo is a respectable business."

"No doubt."

The man speaks in a very exaggerated way, shouting and wrinkling up his face and waving his arms.

"I am the famous cicerone who shows off the town."

"Indeed."

"The people are very ignorant here, they don't know a good thing from a bad one."

"Well, there must be all kinds."

"No, señor, there are not; here everybody is very ignorant and they don't know a good thing from a bad one."

"All right, if you say so."

"My name is Julio Vacas but they call me Portillo, Littlegate. In this town every mother's son has a nickname, nobody escapes from it. Here we have a Foxgelder, a Faggot, and a Scorcher. There's a Pillarhead, a Coastwise, a Skewerer, and a Piss-a-bed. There's a Fried Monkey and a Bighead, a Mohammed and an Eternal Father, a Broth-and-Water and a Skidface, a Meringue and a Smoked Kid, a Friar-come-lately, a Rebel, a Holy Smoke, a Lame Duck, a Heelstamper, a Sharpy, and a Pilate; here, my dear sir, we don't miss a trick."

"So I see."

"And the people in the towns around here call us all clowns and drunkards."

The man speaks all his sentences very rapidly, as if he were reciting a lesson from memory, stopping only to breathe and to laugh a little rabbity laugh. The man knows he has to speak his piece, come what may, and he doesn't care whether it makes sense or not.

"But you know what I say? What I say is, life is like that."

The man smiles, takes a step backward and strikes the studied pose of an actor.

> "In this humble shop of mine
> Every blessed thing you'll find;
> Baskets, shoes, and pottery
> All as tempting as can be."

Julio Vacas is radiant with joy, you can see it in his face. To be sure, he must not find a person as patient as the traveler every day.

"Do you like that verse?"

"Yes, indeed; it's very pretty."

"Well, I made it up all by myself. I know others too; I've made up lots more verses."

"Really?"

"Yes, señor; do you think I'm an ignorant man?"

"I? Heaven forbid!"

The man smiles again.

"Yes, señor, I've made up others, lots of others; I have them all written down. A man gets nowhere if he's not orderly, don't you agree?"

"Of course."

"Then listen to this one that I dedicated to the Blessed Virgin Mary, Mother of Our Lord Jesus Christ."

"Let's hear it."

Portillo became transfigured again.

"Brihuega folk are blessed
 Since in the days that were
We found our little Virgin
 And raised a church to her."

The traveler is about to say something, but the secondhand dealer interrupts him with a gesture that seems to say, "Just a minute, one little minute." He throws up his arms again and bursts into verse anew:

"In this our worthy city
 Three shining gems we own;
The Virgin's temple, Philip's church,
 The Gate of Cozagón."

When he has finished he scratches his head violently.

"Eh?"

"Well, well."

The traveler goes into the shop with Julio Vacas at his heels. The shop has everything; it is like an Oriental bazaar; porcelain lamps, pottery cuspidors, glass inkwells, old silver coins, pictures, books, harness, bronze oil lamps, sheepskins, peacock feathers, fine but mended platters, old coats, a collection of Argentine stamps, two packages of German marks of the First World War, weighing half-a-kilo each. Julio Vacas, alias Portillo, keeps on talking to the traveler.

"Are you fond of reading?"

"Yes, occasionally I read something."

"Then I'm going to give you two books I'm very proud of. They're very old, they were written by real scholars. I don't want anything for them; don't let your right hand know what your left is doing, that's my motto. I'm going to make you a present of them. They're books for the health; you look a trifle pale."

While the odds-and-ends dealer searches for the books the traveler passes the time looking at the walls.

"Here they are."

"Why, thanks."

The traveler fishes two pesetas out of his pocket.

"No; I don't charge for things like this."

"Excuse me, these two pesetas aren't for the books, I realize they're worth more; these two pesetas are a gift."

"Oh, that's another story."

Julio Vacas puts away the two pesetas and the traveler leafs through the books. One is called *Practical Treatise on Gout* and is dated in 1791 at Alcalá, at the Press of the Royal University. It was written in the French language by M. Coste, advisor and senior physician to the Guards of His Majesty the King of Prussia; the Spanish translation was done by Don Ramón Tomé, professor of surgery at the Court, who added to it a *Treatise on Mineral Waters*. The other is called *Curative Medicine, or Purgation*, and was written by M. Leroy, a consulting surgeon of Paris. The frontispiece bears two lines which read, "Who carries me in his pocket carries the doctor with him." The book is dated at Valencia in 1828, at the printing shop of José Ferrer de Orga, and has a portrait of the author with a half-border in English lettering which says, "M. Leroy, Promoter of Curative Medicine."

"How about it, do you like my little books?"

"Yes, they seem interesting."

"Well, I had them there, waiting to find someone who deserved to own them. Give them to me, I'm going to sign them for you."

The traveler looks at Julio Vacas and Julio Vacas displays some tiny, pointed greenish teeth as he signs the books with infinite care. Julio Vacas has been smiling.

"I've showed the town to all the distinguished visitors."

"Do many come?"

"Yes, señor, and very important ones. Years ago, before the airplanes, I showed the King of France around the town."

"Really?"

"Yes, señor, precisely so! It was during a trip he took incognito, absolutely incognito."

Julio Vacas lowers his voice, raises his eyebrows and speaks into the traveler's ear.

"It was about the time Don Niceto Alcalá Zamora was elected President. I'm going to tell you something that maybe you don't know, something that hasn't circulated much. You'll know it now but you'll act as if you don't, eh?"

"All right."

"Well, he and Don Niceto were cousins!"

"I'll be damned!"

"Yes, señor. And naturally, since Don Niceto was a Republican, he had to make the trip incognito for fear of what people would say. I know all this from excellent sources."

Julio Vacas raises his voice again, after winking at the traveler.

"He was a man it was a pleasure to talk to; a very intelligent man, tall and well-dressed. You could see right away that he was a king from some foreign country."

"Well, well—"

"And when he left he said to me, 'Portillo, take this and go and get drunk in my honor.' And he went and gave me ten pesetas. What a binge I had!"

"I'll bet you did!"

"You only had to look at him to know he was a man of position."

Julio Vacas rolls up his eyes as if remembering.

"When I told him that one about Our Lady, Saint Philip, and the Gate of Cozagón he took out his wallet and gave me another peseta."

The traveler reflects that he had better not try to compete with the King of France. Julio Vacas, who doesn't know what the traveler is thinking, continues to recite:

"A little old lady of modest means
Gorged on a hundred-odd sardines.
She spent the night, 'mid moans and groans,
Plucking her rectum clean of bones."

"Did you tell that one to the King of France too?"

"No, señor; not that one, I thought it up afterwards."

"You thought up that one?"

"Yes, señor, I swear I did. It has spread a lot, with the speed of light, but the original person who thought it up was your humble servant."

Julio Vacas gazes at the floor as he says these last words.

"It's a pity you didn't tell it to him; maybe he would have given you another peseta."

"He undoubtedly would have."

Portillo changed his tone of voice, as if trying to pick up the thread of something he had said before.

"By the way, did you notice that in the poem I used a very polite word, 'rectum'?"

"Yes, I noticed."

The secondhand dealer is lost in thought and says absently, as though talking to himself, "What a fine memory I have of Don Luis!"

"His name was Don Luis?"

"Yes, señor; Don Luis Capet."

Then, with his hands in his trouser pockets and his shoulders hunched, he asks as he walks up and down the shop, "Do you know what might have become of him?"

"No, not a thing; I don't keep up with what happens in France."

"Same with me . . ."

Julio Vacas goes to the door and looks out on the street.

"What a fine gentleman! He didn't seem like a Frenchman!"

Julio Vacas, who has a sort of vague resemblance to a guerrilla leader, puts both hands to his head like an operatic tenor. His appearance is impressively ridiculous, so ridiculous that it is positively frightening.

"What a great figure of History!"

Julio Vacas looks at the traveler out of the corner of his eye, pretending not to. The traveler doesn't react at all when he hears about the figure of History.

The dealer turns on his smile again.

"Well, what does it matter? None of us can cope with Fate!"

"How true."

"Let's talk about something else. Have you seen the garden of the factory?"

"No, I haven't seen it yet."

"Don't miss it; it's really magnificent, you'll see."

The traveler takes his leave of Julio Vacas, alias Portillo, sitting listlessly in a tavern in front of two glasses of wine. As he left the shop, Julio Vacas had shouted, in a great resounding thundering voice, "María! María!"

And when María appeared from a side street he had told her, "Keep an eye on the business, I'm going out with this gentleman for a while."

Once in the tavern the traveler had tried to dissuade Julio Vacas.

"Thanks a lot, but don't bother. I can get to the garden very easily by myself. Sometimes I'm—how can I explain?—a rather solitary man."

Julio Vacas kept his eyes fixed on the counter and merely said very low, in a sad, gloomy voice filled with bitterness, "As you like."

The traveler, who as always realized too late that he had been cruel, gave him two more pesetas. Julio Vacas put them in his pocket almost without moving.

"Thanks."

"That's all right. After all, I'm not the King of France."

Julio Vacas, with a glass of white wine in his hand, let fall these words, "I've always said there weren't many like him."

The traveler goes on his way. An old woman with glasses is sitting on a wooden bench in the shade of the arcades, knitting. Beside her a child is crying disconsolately and stamping on the ground. You would think he had just had a tremendous spanking.

"What's the matter with him?"

"Nothing; he's just hot."

An old man is eating smoked sardines and a chunk of bread. He is sitting at the foot of a column with his donkey beside him. The donkey is old too, with a gray hide and sad meditative eyes. He has a bloody harness-sore, plagued with flies, on his hairy neck, and under the saddle you can see that his back is sunken by the years. The old man raises his head when he sees the traveler go by. The traveler greets him.

"Good afternoon."

"May God give us many another."

The old man has white hair and shining blue eyes. He is threadbare, with his flesh poorly and thinly covered, but he does not look like a beggar. The traveler thinks about those poor folk who don't give the impression of being beggars, of the poor of whom it might be said that they are all gentlemen of rank who have come down in the world, as proud and resigned as heroes in misfortune.

The traveler feels curiosity toward the old man with the donkey. The traveler isn't used to beggars with blue eyes and an old mount, wandering beggars who travel tirelessly from one place to another, who today eat smoked sardines in Brihuega; yesterday, perhaps, they woke up fasting in an oak grove, or lunched on salt beef or garlic soup in Villaviciosa or Valdesaz; and tomorrow, like the birds of the heavens, they will trust in what God may provide.

"Are you on the road?"

"Yes, señor."

"Going far?"

"Pshaw, that's as you might look at it; I'm in no hurry."

The old man puts one hand to his brow as he talks with the traveler.

"You too?"

"Yes, me too. I'm leaving tonight."

"God willing . . ."

"That's right, God willing."

The garden of the factory, surrounded by high walls bristling with vegetation, is reached by a steep luminous empty road. The traveler goes in and a dog barks at him. A man comes out.

"Did you want to see the gardens?"

The man seems used to showing the place; he must have asked that question many times now in the course of his life. He says "the gardens" instead of "the garden," which would be less elegant, and always lets the traveler go ahead of him when they cross a threshold. The factory doesn't manufacture anything. At one time, the traveler seems to remember having heard, it manufactured cloth. In a great empty workroom reposes a carriage covered with dust and cobwebs. The traveler and the guard go through a square cobbled patio like that of a convent, with brambles and nettles in the corners and a basin of greenish water that bubbles slightly. The basin is surrounded by iris. A few doves are pecking at the ground. On the other side of the patio, in a meadow with a railing at the far side, a meadow that slopes down giving a view of the city, two Swiss cows are grazing in the shade of some fruit trees. They have short blunt horns and a faraway, vague, stupid look.

From the patio there is a little door leading into the garden. The garden is breathtaking. Julio Vacas was right, it *is* a magnificent garden. The guard fondly shows off his garden.

"This is the greenhouse. Go on in."

The traveler doesn't go in; he doesn't much care for greenhouses.

"Now that there's so much rain we can't keep the paths clean, there's grass growing everywhere."

The guard doesn't realize that the garden is even more enchanting with a little grass growing in the paths.

"Look, what a beautiful bay tree."

The garden of the factory is a romantic garden, a garden to die in when one is very young, of love or desperation, of consumption and nostalgia. Beside the graceful almond tree, which seems like a dead young girl, grows the solemn cypress, so like a living penitent. Behind the pruned and shaped box hedges bloom the pagan roses of Jericho. Near the perennial myrtle the wild honeysuckle is pale by contrast. The traveler walks among the rhododendrons and in spite of himself his mind is flooded with delicate, unhealthy lines from Shelley; wine, honey, new moon, dog-rose . . .

"No, it's better not."

The traveler passes a hand over his brow and rubs his eyes.

"In this pool, before the airplanes, there always used to be goldfish."

The traveler is not listening. He goes up to the high overlook with its garland of tea roses and gazes down toward the valley. The river Tajuña runs at the bottom of it, and on its banks is the road the traveler will take at nightfall, either upriver behind Masegoso or downriver behind the highway to Budia.

5. FROM THE TAJUÑA TO THE CIFUENTES

LATE in the afternoon the traveler goes down to the river. To his left, up the Tajuña, goes the road to Masegoso and Cifuentes; to the right, down the Tajuña, the one to Archilla or Budia. The traveler can't make up his mind and sits down in the ditch, his back to the town and his face toward the river, to await the moment of decision. Leaning back on his pack he feels comfortable and rested. The pack is just the right size; it reaches down to the small of his back and gives him a tall, friendly support, a little hard perhaps.

Some small red clouds, elongated like little snakes, are slowly crossing the western sky; their edges are precise and well-defined. People say that red clouds at sunset presage heat for the next day. The river runs noisily and rapidly through the meadows and the little birds of the afternoon chirp on its banks, the last frogs of the afternoon are croaking. It is cool, sitting here by the side of the highway in the shade of an elm, after a hot day during which one has walked a number of leagues and then footed it from one side to the other of a large and newly discovered town. A dragonfly passes with its jerky flight. Two young girls go by, riding on a gentle gelded donkey who walks slowly with his head bent forward. The girls sit very close together, laughing loudly, with poppies in their hair. An occasional peasant who has spent the day farming his land—hoeing beans, weeding onions, watering lettuce—comes back toward Brihuega with his hoe on his shoulder, his face tanned by the air and the sun, his noble, classic forehead shining with sweat. In front of the traveler on the bank of the river a woman is cutting rushes with a knife. The woman had arrived holding a little girl by the hand. The child is barefoot, her arms are bare, and she has a purple bow as big as a bat on her untidy blonde hair. When they get to the river, while the mother heaps up the rush stalks, the child silently cuts iris. Eventually she has a pile as big as she is, a pile she'll never be able to carry. Swarms of bees are buzzing in the hives of an apiary not ten steps away from the traveler, and the countryside has a deep penetrating distant odor which is almost painful.

The traveler's eyelids are heavy. He may even have slept for a moment, a light sleep, without realizing it. He is immobile, perfectly at ease; he doesn't feel his legs, which lie in the same position he took when he sat down. It is neither chilly nor warm.

A little rabbit-hunting dog trots along the ditch. The traveler lights a cigar that he bought in Guadalajara. The smoke rises slowly, straight up, occasionally forming tenuous blue spirals. A light-colored cat stares at the traveler from a tree. Not a breath of air is stirring.

Calmly and contemplatively, a man walking behind a donkey comes down the hill. The man walks like a knight in retreat. His head is high and the look in his eyes is vague and absent-minded. He has blue eyes. The donkey is an old one with a gray hide and a sagging back. By looking closely one can see a bloody sore, black with flies, on his shaggy neck.

The traveler feels his heart leap in his breast. As the old man comes closer he shouts at him.

"Eh!"

And the old man, who has recognized him, stops the donkey with his voice.

"Whoa, Gorrión!"

The donkey stops and the old man sits down beside the traveler.

"It was a good afternoon, after all."

"Yes, indeed."

The traveler offers his tobacco pouch to the old man.

"Cigarette?"

"I never turn up my nose at that."

The old man rolls a thick generous cigarette, a friendly cigarette which he wraps with extreme care as if he enjoyed doing it. He says nothing for a few moments and then, as he puts out with his fingers the long orange wick of his primitive lighter, asks almost hesitantly, "Are you going to Cifuentes?"

"I don't know; I hadn't made up my mind to start off. Are you?"

"Yes, that's where I'm going. Cifuentes is a good town, a very rich town."

"So they tell me."

"Well, it's the truth. Haven't you ever been to Cifuentes?"

"No, I never have."

"Then come along with me; the people there are good to us wandering folk."

The old man spoke his words looking vaguely toward the horizon.

"Good tobacco!"

"Yes, when you feel like smoking, it's not bad."

The two friends take a drink out of the canteen and get up. The donkey Gorrión carries the traveler's pack. They walk only a short while before night falls, then have a bite to eat and in the last faint light of the evening look for a place to sleep.

On the grass at the foot of the adobe walls of a flour mill—the traveler's gray cotton blanket under them, the old man's heavy checkered woolen blanket over them—the two friends lie on their backs, shoulder to shoulder, with their caps on and their heads resting on the knapsack and saddlebag. The old man has a rich, warm, mellow odor which positively invites sleep. Gorrión the donkey, his front feet hobbled with a rope, stands unmoving, indifferent as if dead, like a statue lost among the shadows of a garden.

The crickets are singing and a dog is barking, not angrily but long and reluctantly, as though obeying a worn-out commandment. A little cart passes along the highway, pulled by a nimble mule who goes trotting along making his harness bells tinkle. In the distance the monotonous bell of a milk cow can be heard. A toad is peeping in the fallow field on the other side of the road.

The traveler sleeps like a log until the small hours of the morning, when the cocks crow for the first time and the old man wakes him up by passing some blades of grass over his face.

"Hail Mary."

"Conceived without sin."

"Shall we go?"

"Sure."

The old man gets up and stretches. He folds the blanket carefully, loads it on the donkey and yawns.

"I always start after twelve o'clock, when the cock crows. It's better walking then, don't you think? The morning was made for walking and the night for sleeping, I always say."

"Yes, I think so too."

The night is still dark. It is cool and the walking is pleasant.

"Now that we've slept for a night under the same blanket and kept each other warm we must be friends by this time, wouldn't you say?"

The old man stops and then adds, "Well, that's what I say anyway!"

The traveler thinks so too, but he doesn't answer.

"After all, d'you know for sure when we'll each go our own way?"

"No."

The friends eat a mouthful of bread and sausage as they go along. The traveler walks in silence, listening to the old man singing under his breath a gay and carefree song which begins, "Girls from Torrebeleña, girls from Fuencemillán." Gorrión the donkey walks a few steps ahead, unhobbled, moving his ears rhythmically. Sometimes he stops and pulls up a thistle or a poppy from the ditch with his enormous teeth.

The traveler and the old man talk about the donkey.

"For a beast, he's as old as I am for a man. But only God knows which of us is to die first."

In the darkness, the blanket over his shoulders, the old man rambles on, his voice slightly muffled and his appearance ghostly.

"He always goes loose, as you see, and a few steps ahead."

The old man squeezes the traveler's arm.

"And when the night comes that I lie like a dog in the road, I'll say to him with all the strength I have left, 'Get up, Gorrión!' and Gorrión will keep walking until day comes and someone finds him. Maybe he'll last another four or five years."

The old man stops talking for an instant and then his voice changes; now it is strangely sharp.

"There's a paper sewed inside the saddle that says, 'Take me, my master is dead.' The druggist in Tenebrón, near Ciudad Rodrigo, wrote it out for me in fine round letters two years before the war."

They go on in silence for a while and then the old man bursts out laughing.

"Let's have another little drink—so far, I'm still pretty tough; nobody's going to read the druggist's writing yet!"

"May that be the truth!"

"And I hope you'll still be around too."

A dog comes growling out of the fields. The old man throws a few stones at him and the dog runs away. He has a big head and is wearing a spiked collar, on which one of the old man's hits clangs like metal on cobblestone.

"Barriopedro is over there, on the bank of that little stream. Sometimes the stream carries a little water; it probably has quite a bit now. It starts up in some lands called El Villar."

A short distance farther on, near the highway, is Valderrebollo.

"There's a road from here that goes to Olmeda."

Dawn is just breaking. The sky is lightening above some dry, earth-colored, almost reddish hills behind Valderrebollo.

"Those are called Las Morras."

The friends have been walking a long time now—perhaps three or four hours—when they go through Mascgoso.

"As far as I'm concerned we can stop. I'm in no hurry."

"Are you getting tired?"

"No, not I. If you want, we'll go on to Cifuentes."

Masegoso, lying at a crossroads, is a big dusty town, silver-colored with touches of gold in the morning light. The men are going out to the fields, with the pair of mules in front of them and the little dog running behind. A few women dragging hoes are going out to work in the garden plots.

Gorrión the donkey, the old man, and the traveler cross the bridge over the Tajuña. A fisherman is walking up and down the bank of the river. The town is off at one side with the sun behind it.

At about eight-thirty or nine the friends make a halt, already in sight of Moranchel. Moranchel is on the left of the Cifuentes road, at some two hundred paces from the highway. It is a gloomy, dark town that seems to have no business being surrounded by green fields. The old man sits down in the ditch and the traveler lies on his back and looks up at some little clouds, graceful as doves, which are floating in the sky. A stork flies past, not very high, with a snake in its beak. Some partridge fly up from a bed of thyme. An adolescent goatherd and a member of his flock are sinning one of the oldest of sins in the shade of a hawthorn tree blooming with tiny sweet-smelling flowers, white as orange blossoms.

Lolling on his back, the traveler goes to sleep in the sun thinking about the Old Testament.

A racketing, dirty, misshapen truck goes by, raising a cloud of dust. When the traveler gets up, the old man is sewing a button on his jacket.

At noon the friends arrive in Cifuentes, a fine, cheerful-looking town with a good supply of water, a town whose women have deep dark eyes, whose well-stocked places of business sell nickel-plated beds, liqueur sets with a decanter and six glasses and a mirrored tray, and wholesome beatific pictures in a hundred colors, representing the Last Supper or a Tyrolean mill surrounded by lofty snow-covered peaks. Behind the town lies the hill of La Horca, a height which is topped by a level place as flat as a plate. The traveler is given to understand that long ago, when the simple folk who like a bit of blood now and then needed to be entertained (bullfights hadn't been invented yet), the flat space on top of La Horca was used to carry out sentences on those condemned to death. The traveler reflects that the site wasn't a bad choice; there's no doubt that the hill of La Horca has a beautiful view. The traveler thinks too that it's a pity they don't put up a gallows on the hill of La Horca; it would have made a pretty sight.

At the edge of town, near the river, is the harness shop of "The Rat," a little, motley, enchanting place; a regular medieval workshop, cheerful and exposed to all the winds of Heaven like an open-air market. The Rat's name is Félix Marco Laina. The Rat is a clever man, a man who knows how to make the best of a nickname, to squeeze the good out of it as one would squeeze a lemon. In his shop, surrounded by thongs, packsaddles, and riding saddles, the Rat is a sort of consul of the Alcarria and his workshop is a general bureau of people's comings and goings. Sooner or later everybody winds up passing through the Rat's harness shop, in search of a cinch or a saddle pad, in quest of a crupper, on the trail of a girth or a mule yoke.

The traveler presents Gorrión the donkey with some saddle padding, and Gorrión the donkey switches his tail, nervous as a child, while they put it on him.

The friends go down toward the river meadow, in the opposite direction from town. They are going to eat and then take a little nap at the fountain of Piojo, which has clear fresh water that is famous in the district. Between the fountain of Piojo and the river the garden plots flourish greenly. Above the highway to Gárgoles the walls of a ruined castle can be seen. The old man doesn't know whose castle it was. A woman passing by doesn't know either.

"Now it belongs to a marchioness."

At three o'clock in the afternoon the traveler retraces his steps and goes into Cifuentes, where he has a friend he wants to visit. The old man stays at the fountain of Piojo, digesting his meal in the shade.

"We'll see each other later."

"All right."

The traveler's friend in the town is named Arbeteta. Arbeteta is a vigorous gentleman of the old school, past fifty or maybe even past sixty, but robust and healthy as can be, with half-a-dozen grown children and a house with three French balconies as graceful as the loges in an opera house.

"Cifuentes is the capital of the Alcarria. The Alcarria is known for its honey, and the most honey is to be found in the Cifuentes district—in Huétor, Ruguilla, Oter and Carrascosa."

The traveler's friend speaks of Cifuentes with pride. As they walk through the town he explains all its antiquities. The traveler learns that the castle was built by Don Juan Manuel* and the church by a mistress of Alfonso the Wise named Doña Mayor. The traveler recalls vaguely that in a book he read years ago, Don Juan Manuel was referred to as turbulent and quarrelsome. As for Doña Mayor, the traveler has never heard of her in his life.

Many of the doors in the town have pretty, very artistic ironwork, with knockers and doorknobs of black iron and decorations for the keyhole in different shapes: a heart, a cloverleaf, a fleur-de-lis, an arabesque.

The river Cifuentes has its source right under the houses. No sooner has it begun than it turns a mill; the whole town is built on a spring. The Cifuentes is a precocious river, small in size but large in volume, which flows into the Tajo at Trillo; its course is little more than two leagues but it runs full of water, fuller no doubt than many longer rivers. In its short course the Cifuentes runs from waterfall to waterfall; it leaps over the stones at least half a hundred times.

A flock of graceful tame ducks is swimming in the millpond; each has an arched and shining tailfeather, a gray feather with blue and green and red glints in it. A few ducks are sleeping on the bank, some standing up and some huddled with their heads under their wings. Others are walking about, quacking and rolling from side to side like sailors. The traveler stands looking over the railing of the bridge, a yard or so from the water, and throws them a few crumbs of bread. The ducks rush up hastily, beating their wings on the water. The sleeping ones on the bank wake up with a great flutter of feathers, look around for a moment, and then start swimming too.

As they stroll from one side of the town to the other, Arbeteta tells the traveler the legend of the Fountain of Gold, at the foot of the hill called San Cristóbal on the road to Ruguilla. It is a

*Don Juan Manuel (1284–1348), a nephew of King Alfonso the Wise; courtier and author. [Translator's note.]

very literary tale, too literary perhaps, of Moors and Christians, of gold nuggets as big as cherries, and of virgin princesses, pale, beautiful, and mysterious as the moon. The tale has a charming flavor of fable about it and the traveler thinks, contrary to his custom, of the minstrels of the Middle Ages who played their lutes in the ladies' courtyard of every castle, and who were flogged till the blood came in the knights' courtyard if they played out of tune.

Sitting in the sun, an invalid boy is reading Andersen's fairy tales out of a handsome book with stiff covers. As the traveler goes by, the child raises his head and gazes at him. He has dark curly hair, dark eyes, white skin, and a charming, prematurely embittered smile. He is paralyzed from the waist down, seated always in his little wicker chair. The traveler asks him how he is and the boy says fine, thanks, taking the sun a little. The mother comes to the door. The traveler asks her for a drink of water and the boy's mother invites him to come in and offers him a glass of wine. Then she tells him that the boy's name is Paquito; that he was born normal, a lovely child, but he got crooked very soon, he has infantile paralysis, and some nights when they put him to bed they can hear him crying softly for a long time until he goes to sleep. She tells the traveler too that she tries to bear it as best she can, believing that it is a cross which the Lord has sent her.

"We had two others and both of them died, not as babies either. My husband says, what sin must we have committed."

The woman's eyes are sad. She stares at the wall and adds, "Well, after all, this is the cross that has fallen to me."

When he gets to the plaza the traveler sees his friend the old man, with Gorrión the donkey beside him.

"I was waiting for you."

"Really?"

"Yes, señor, I wanted to say goodbye."

"But where are you going?"

"I'm not going, I'm staying. I've got a job of work to do and I'll stay till I finish it, three or four days. I suppose you'll keep going."

The traveler hesitates for a moment.

"Yes, I'll keep walking; nobody's given me any work."

The old man speaks, looking at Gorrión's head, pretending to be offhand, as though he wanted to make the words sound less important.

"It's little enough, but half of it's yours if you want."

"No, thanks just the same; in times like these there's not enough to share."

"As you like."

The old man and the traveler look at each other.

"Which way do you think you'll go?"

"I had thought of going down to Trillo."

The old man and the traveler shake hands and say goodbye.

"Well, maybe we'll see each other."

"That's as God wills."

"And if we don't see each other—"

"If we don't see each other, good luck."

The old man, who had stood up, sits down again while the traveler, who feels a little depressed—why not admit it?—starts up a narrow street where two women are walking with their pitchers on their arms.

The friend asks the traveler, "Who's that?"

And the traveler tells him, "An old friend of mine, a very fine person. His name is Jesús and he's from over toward Belmonte, from a town called Villaescusa, and he goes about making his way in the world just as I'm doing now."

In the parish church of El Salvador there is a pulpit of jasper or alabaster which must be worth a fortune, a pulpit of great excellence. It has some very carefully sculptured figures and is finished off at the bottom by a head with two faces like Janus', only these are a man's and a woman's. The priest tells the traveler the recent history of the pulpit.

"After the war I had a terrible time finding it. Finally it turned up in Madrid, in a museum. At first they didn't want to give it to me, they tried to give me another one instead. One day I went with a man from here who has a truck, I took my stand at the door of the museum and I said, 'Bring out that pulpit, it's mine.'

I loaded it on the truck and there it is."

The priest is courageous and determined, a congenial and hardworking priest who is proud of his pulpit; as soon as he found it he brought it home and that was that.

The church has a door that leads to a patio with a grape arbor and a few trees. The patio also gives access to the priest's house.

"This is the best arrangement for me. Do I want to take the air a bit? Well, I just take my walk here and then I only have to go out on the street in case of necessity."

The priest's house is clean and light, with well-scrubbed wood floors and whitewashed walls. The priest takes the traveler to the door. They have to go down quite a number of steps because the ground is uneven; the door which leads in from the patio is at the level of the second-story windows on the street side. At the door they say farewell.

"Well, Father, goodbye, it's been a pleasure."

"Goodbye, my friend, no trouble; the pleasure was mine, best of luck."

The traveler goes off with his friend, and looks back as he turns the corner. The priest is standing in the middle of the street waving goodbye.

A dog is sniffing at a heap of garbage. Two immense earthen jars are lying empty in a corner, out in the sun.

"Now let's have something to eat, if you like, and then we'll go to the house they call the Synagogue. It's very ancient, as you'll see."

As was to be expected, the traveler thinks it a very fine thing to have a bite to eat. He is hungry, and in Arbeteta's house he has a glass of thick milk the color of lard and a piece of close-grained, soft white bread two handbreadths across. With his stomach full the traveler turns a bit sentimental. He notices it and pulls himself up short.

"How about seeing the Synagogue?"

"Let's go, if you want to."

After his snack the traveler had begun to think about whistling birds, dear little butterflies, wandering children, and other such trifles. That's the trouble with a full stomach; it fills one's mind with ideas worthy of an old-maid Sunday school teacher.

The house called the Synagogue is a two-story house with rather small windows and a columned patio. In the patio is a well with a high curbstone, covered with planks. A few hens are pecking in some manure and a pig roots in the ground, grunting.

The traveler's friend calls, "Come on out, María, we've come to see your house."

The owner emerges, wiping her hands on her apron.

"There's not much to see. It's a poor house, as you can tell."

Some swallows are flying swift as lightning across the patio. They have their nests in the beams and under the capitals of the columns. There are marks too, a little more than halfway up the wall, of other nests that must have fallen down one fine day without anyone's having disturbed them.

"You know, swallows are just like people, there are smart ones and stupid ones. Just look how those other nests have never fallen!"

After explaining about the swallows, the owner brings two stools out of the house so that the traveler and his friend can sit down. In the cool of the afternoon one feels very much at ease, sitting in a patio smoking and talking to the owner of a synagogue.

"Did you know that once upon a time this was all full of Jews?"

"I know it to my sorrow, may God strike them dead! The murderers of Our Lord!"

As always, the traveler doesn't realize he has put his foot in it until he's in belly-deep. Then he consoles himself by thinking that the woman must know that people from Cifuentes—and from Alovera and Taracena and Torija and Uceda—are called Jews by way of insult in all the country around here. And they call people from Romancos perjurers, which is worse still. The traveler thinks too that, true or untrue, it's the custom.

He gets up, then, and talks of the harvest, which is safe conversation this year, of the weather and of how fine the hens are; they are already disappearing up some poles into the henhouse. Two doves are sleeping on top of a woodpile. A child comes in with his primer under his arm.

"Niño, say how-do-you-do to this gentleman!"

"Good afternoon, señor."

The traveler, to get into his good graces, gives the child a small coin.

"Niño, what do you say?"

"Many thanks, señor."

The child is scarcely a hand's breadth away from the traveler, staring at him fixedly, breathing on him. His breath smells like a baby calf's, a little sucking calf's.

"Do you know your letters?"

"Yes, señor."

"What's this letter?"

"An *e*."

"And this one?"

"An *m*."

"Fine. Do you know your rules of arithmetic?"

"No, señor, I don't know them."

Back on the street again, the light is different. The sun has set over the hills behind the fountain of Piojo, and the houses begin to take on a more subdued, duskier tone. Tied to a ring in a doorway, switching his tail joyfully, is Gorrión the donkey, who has had a fairly restful day. Through the open door one can see the patio where the old man whom the traveler came upon in Brihuega eating bread and smoked sardines at the foot of a column under the arches, is cleaning out a cesspool: the job of work.

Night falls rather quickly on Cifuentes. Above the town the hill of La Horca shows its solitary silhouette. The bell of El Salvador, in a tower which a bomb cut down the middle like a knife, has called to evening prayer some time since. The traveler reflects that tomorrow is another day.

6. ALONG THE CIFUENTES TO THE TAJO

EARLY next morning the traveler sets out from Cifuentes on the road to Trillo, with the river on his right and the castle of Don Juan Manuel on his left.

When he has walked a little way he can see on the horizon, stubby and isolated, the hills called Las Tetas de Viana. And as he tops a gentle rise a short time later, he sees Gargolillos too with its pointed tower and Gárgoles with its square one. Some people call Gargolillos Upper Gárgoles, and Gárgoles Lower Gárgoles. Both towns are on the banks of the Cifuentes, Gargolillos a trifle off the highway at the end of a very pretty road lined with walls and with brambles.

It is slightly chilly and walking is a pleasure. A slender, almost imperceptible ribbon of mist hangs over the river. Starlings and swifts are on the wing; a black-and-white magpie hops from stone to stone and a lark is singing in the fields. The light morning wind caresses the countryside and the air is clean, clear, transparent, diaphanous.

Just behind the brow of a little hill, Cifuentes disappears. The road runs among sparse and isolated poplar groves. Between the road and the river, gardens are turning green. On the other side, the earth becomes dry and hard again, dusky in color. On the dry lands are flocks of sheep, white and black—more precisely, a dark reddish-brown—all mixed together, and on the side where the water is, there are women and children working the fields.

The road is empty; no one is coming or going. The traveler passes a big stone house that seems to be abandoned. It has some orchard plots around it and a little garden. At the gate is a sign which reads, "No admittance. Private property."

A man is sitting on a milestone arranging a tray of trinkets.

"You coming from Cifuentes?"

"Yes."

"How're things there?"

"Fine, I guess!"

The man makes a gesture of displeasure.

"All right then, I won't go."

"But why not, for Heaven's sake?"

"What d'you expect? I won't go. Nobody tells me the truth."

The peddler has perfectly naked eyelids, without a single lash, and a wooden leg crudely fixed to the stump with thongs. He has a scar all across his forehead and a bluish, almost white film on one eye. He is short, skinny as a rail, and has a nasty disposition.

"Nobody tells me the truth. I disgust everybody. D'you know what they call me in Guadalajara?"

"No."

"Well, they call me Old Crap, what d'you think of that?"

"Well, good Lord! I think it's ugly, but what do you want me to say?"

"The bastards! They ought to be skinned alive! Hey, can you give me a bit of tobacco for my pipe?"

The traveler offers his pouch.

"Yes, with pleasure, have some."

"Why did you say 'with pleasure'?"

The traveler hesitates before he answers.

"Because it's true. Go on, light your pipe."

"All right, all right, no need to put yourself out, damn everybody! It's hard to believe you'd be so high-and-mighty about giving me a little tobacco. Hey, are you from Aranzueque?"

"No, why?"

"I dunno, just seemed to me you were kind of hungry-looking."

The man glances at his tray and straightens up the colored ribbons, the slips of paper with fortunes on them, the gilded metal combs as polished and shiny as mirrors.

"Don't sell a damn thing!"

"Yes, times are bad."

The man raises his head and looks the traveler in the eye.

"And you complain, tall as you are and walking on two feet?"

The traveler is beginning to think that the ribbon-man has a disconcerting way of putting things.

"I had a great fortune, an inheritance, stolen from me."

"Is that so?"

"Yes; señor; or don't you believe me?"

"Of course, of course, why shouldn't I believe you?"

"Well, it was the fortune of the Viceroy of Peru. You've heard tell of the Viceroy of Peru?"

"Yes, often."

"Well, he left me his entire fortune. On his deathbed he called the notary and right in front of him he wrote on a paper: "I, Don Jerónimo de Villegas y Martín, Viceroy of Peru, do hereby will all my fortune, present and future, to my nephew Don Estanislao de Kostka Rodríguez y Rodríguez, alias Old Crap." I know it off by heart. The paper is locked up in Rome because I've had such a hard time of it, I don't trust anybody any more except the Pope."

The peddler stood up and went on, "They stole my inheritance from me, and left me in the utmost indingance."

It took the traveler a few moments to realize that he had meant to say "indigence."

"But what I say is, what good will it do them if on the Day of Judgment the truth will all come to light?"

"Indeed, that's so."

"Of course it is, man, of course it is! Those people in Guadalajara, they say one thing at night and a different thing in the morning! But we'll see what happens on the Day of Judgment. Hey, shall we get going?"

"All right."

The man walks painfully, limping.

"This pegleg of mine is too long. Hey, isn't your pack pretty heavy?"

"Yes, a little."

"Why don't you throw it away?"

After an hour's walk, Upper Gárgoles comes into view, on the banks of the Cifuentes and a little off the highway. A man in a beret and scarf and two young women are waiting for the bus to come by. They are the only inhabitants of Gargolillos with whom the traveler has any contact and they certainly have the look of good people, though folk from other towns are apt to call them *lañas,* which means the same as thieves.

The traveler listens to the tale of how the peddler lost his leg.

"Well, I'll tell you. On the day of San Enrique, the year the Republic came in, I said to myself, 'Estanislao, you've got to finish things off. You're a no-good, can't you see you're a no-good?' It was so hot that day, I couldn't stand it. I was in Camporreal. I went over near Arganda and I lay down on the tracks. 'When the train comes along,' I thought, 'off goes Estanislao to another world.' Sure, sure, but . . . ! I was cool as a cucumber, I swear I was, but that was before the train came. When the train showed up I felt like my belly was going to let go. I held on for a while, but when the train was right on top of me I said to myself, 'Get away, Estanislao, it's going to cut you to pieces!' I jumped, but my leg didn't make it. If it hadn't been for some fellows from the sugar factory who picked me up, I would have bled to death like a stuck pig. They took me to the doctor's house and he fixed me up and that's where they gave me the nickname, when they saw the state my pants were in. One of the ones that picked me up was carrying the leg in his hand, still stuck inside the boot, and all he could do was ask, 'Say, what do I do with this thing?' You could tell that the doctor didn't know what to do, because all he said to him was, 'That *thing* is called a leg, you fool, it's called a leg.' "

The traveler thinks it prudent to interrupt. The peddler, as he talks about the leg he left in Arganda, had taken on a mournful air, a crestfallen attitude.

"How would you like to light your pipe again?"

"Sure. Hey, d'you know much about pipes?"

"Not much."

"Then it's hardly worthwhile explaining anything to you. I'll just tell you that this is a Camellia de Luxe, from Paris, France. Damn your ignorance! Hey, d'you know who gave it to me?"

"No."

"Then listen and you'll find out. It was General Weyler, one day in the Paseo de Rosales in Madrid."

The man looked at the traveler with a triumphant air and smiled.

"He, he! So who did you think you were talking to?"

It is eleven o'clock in the morning and the traveler feels hungry.

"Will you swear to me that you're not from Aranzueque?"

"Of course I'll swear, man."

"Well!"

The hawker sat down in the ditch, untied his wooden leg, and lighted his pipe.

"Now then, let's have a bite, shall we? Which d'you rather, do we share or each one eat his own?"

"It's better we share, don't you think?"

"As far as I'm concerned, sure. I think you're getting the worst of the bargain, but what the hell! All I've got is a bit of dried beef."

The two men ate and drank from the pack and canteen of the one who had two good legs. You might think not, but out in the country, sitting on the edge of the road, one sees more clearly than in the city that in this world God arranges things with a good deal of common sense.

The peddler ate like a lion, while the traveler wondered if he wasn't the one from Aranzueque.

"This stuff is really a spread but I like it right out of the can," the ribbon-man said as he devoured a can of *foie gras*. "Leave the bread for later, maybe you'll need it."

With the meal the man became more inquisitive.

"Hey, what d'you do for a living?"

"Well . . . as you see! I just keep going till something turns up."

"No, no, don't act like the Civil Guard was asking you. So, what do you do for a living?"

The traveler didn't know what to answer.

"Spill it, man, spill it! I'm no stool pigeon, and anyway, if you come right down to it, every man jack of us grabs what he can if he gets the chance to. Hell, everybody knows that! On this earth the man that doesn't step lively knows what he can expect. As they say around here,

> When you go to Aleas keep your cape in view
> Or someone from Fuencemillán'll steal it from you.

Now then, if you don't want to talk about it, then don't. See if I care!"

The peddler stopped talking for a moment, took another swallow of wine, and went on, "My mother used to say that in this world the man who eats is the man who steals, and if a man doesn't steal it's because he doesn't know how. So, what *do* you do for a living?"

Just before they got to Lower Gárgoles, after they had walked on for a little while, the peddler took his departure abruptly.

"Want to know something?"

"What?"

"I'm not going to take another step. I'm not going in there."

"Are you tired?"

"No, I'm not tired. I've eaten once today and I'm not going to tempt God. All I go in the towns for is to eat. When I don't behave myself, God punishes me and then I start bleeding from my mouth. Hey, can you give me a little money?"

In Gárgoles the traveler sees some caves with padlocked doors that are used to store wine and potatoes. His friend Estanislao de Kostka Rodríguez y Rodríguez, nephew of the Viceroy of Peru, finds obstacles in his path wherever he goes.

Gárgoles is a town of market gardens, with well-tilled land and industrious people. In Gárgoles the highway comes very close to the river and the two go along together as far as Trillo. Some children who are sitting on a fence survey the traveler. The peasants unkink their spines, straighten up and look at him too. The traveler goes into the little inn which, like the one in Torija, has no name, to rest a while, wash, and wait till lunchtime. The traveler has discovered that in this town, as in all the Alcarria, they don't know the usual word for "inn." He asked for "the inn" and they didn't even understand him. It was when he asked for a lodging that they told him there was no lodging house but there was a place that took travelers. The one in Gárgoles—at the left of the highway as everything in the town is when you approach it from Cifuentes—has a great, nobly ancient, nail-studded door, which looks as if it might be the door of a castle.

The traveler hangs his mirror on a nail right there in the doorway, and shaves off his whiskers. In the mirror he can see that fifteen or twenty people are watching him from a distance.

A mule driver comes out through the entrance way pulling a pair of mules. Some doves are pecking in a pile of chaff. Two dogs are stretched out asleep in the sun. A child with no pants on is squatting on a shed roof doing his necessities. Shrieking like mad, the swallows fly in and out of the entrance way, which is full of nests. The doors of this inn are never closed.

The traveler goes into the dining room, a square chamber with a very high ceiling with chestnut beams showing in it. Decorating the walls are half-a-dozen pictures, of perky bright-colored birds, dead gray rabbits hung up by the feet, scarlet cooked crabs, and silver-colored trout with glassy eyes. A good-looking maid serves at the table; she is in mourning, firm of flesh, and rather dark-skinned. Her black eyes are deep and thoughtful, her mouth large and sensual, her nose slender and well-modeled, her teeth white. The maid of the inn at Gárgoles is impassive and haughty; she neither speaks nor smiles nor glances. She is like a Moorish lady of degree.

A black hound hovers around the traveler as he eats his garlic soup and omelet with canned tuna in it; he is a respectful dog, a thoughtful dog who neither begs nor intrudes, a dog who carries off his poverty with dignity, who eats when somebody gives him something and if nobody does, pretends he doesn't care. Just behind him a hairy reddish dog has slunk into the dining room too; he is a wolfish-looking canine whose look is half-affectionate and half-bewildered. He is a vulgar, ill-bred dog, who growls and shows his teeth when people don't give him anything. He is ravenous, and when the traveler throws him a piece of bread he catches it in the air and goes off to a corner, lies down, and gobbles it. The black dog watches him carefully and never even moves.

After his meal the traveler lights a cigarette, gets up and reads, written in pencil on the whitewashed walls, some phrases like the ones you find in the toilets of secondary schools. There are some to suit all tastes, and in all colors. One of them, written in carefully outlined block letters, says: "Company of Theater and Varieties. Company of Olivares. Two performances 600 pesetas. Smashing success. 13–3–45." It is a very self-satisfied message, optimistic and loaded with euphoria. There is also a woman's head with long flowing hair, signed by Fermín González of Cuenca, a person who puts a beautiful, elegant, pompous flourish under his signature, a challenging lawyer-like flourish.

The traveler loosens his boots, puts his pack under his head for a pillow, wraps himself up in his blanket and lies down to sleep on the floor in a corner. The black dog lies down too, as if to watch over his slumbers. The reddish dog has gone away; he is a dog who lacks character and wisdom and who couldn't have borne lying with his paws folded for an hour or an hour and a half with nothing to do.

From Gárgoles there is a highway which goes directly to Sacedón and which runs for several leagues along the banks of the Tajo. The traveler can't make up his mind whether to go toward Trillo, following the Cifuentes, as he had intended, and going to the end of the river whose source he has already seen, or to take the other road and turn off toward nightfall to sleep in Gualda.

On the outskirts of Gárgoles as the traveler starts for Trillo, a man is beating a big black donkey which kicks like mad and lifts its upper lip, showing its teeth. A woman explains to the traveler that you'd think the donkey was from Hita. Apparently donkeys from Hita have a bad reputation in the region; the same as women from Fraguas.

A little farther on, two men are changing a flat tire on a truck loaded to the brim. The traveler spends all day on the road, and ordinarily he meets no more than two or three buses and a passenger car or light truck now and then.

Gárgoles, left behind now, has sent its people out into the fields. People in Gárgoles are hardworking and determined, some of them maybe a little unfriendly. A drygoods salesman who goes around the region in a cart tells the traveler about a man from Gárgoles who was in a hurry to get rich and who rode a bicycle from La Puerta, some five leagues give or take a bit, loaded with thirteen little kids. When he got to Gárgoles he died of exhaustion; his heart and his liver had ruptured.

"Well, that's the way things go," says the salesman to the traveler, "greed brings its own punishment. And to think that people from Alcocer are called 'barbarians' because they threw their image of Christ in the river!" *

Around Trillo the landscape looks even more fertile. Vegetation flourishes with the aid of the river's water, and the trees rise as gracefully as in Brihuega. This land, since it has water, appears to be very rich; you even see a chestnut tree from time to time. Just on the edge of the town is an extremely neat house all covered with flowers; a mountain climber of long experience, by the name of Schmidt, old now and retired, lives there, cultivating his rosebushes and carnations and working in his orchard. Schmidt, who is thinking about building a house across from the waterfall in the Cifuentes river just before the point where it joins the Tajo, was a famous mountaineer; there is even a path in the Sierra de Guadarrama which bears his name.

The Cifuentes waterfall is a beautiful horsetail shape, some fifteen or twenty meters high, with foaming, noisy water. Beside it innumerable birds sing all day. It is a very pretty spot to build a house, perhaps almost too pretty.

The traveler finds a place to spend the night; he leaves his impedimenta and sets out to take a turn around the town. From the bridge he watches the Tajo flowing by, dirty and muddy and

*The author has explained to us that in the Alcarria this ditty is often sung:

I never saw folk any wilder
Than the people from Alcocer,
They threw their Christ in the river
Because he didn't make it rain!

[Editor's note from original Spanish publication.]

ragged of outline. On its banks a few fishermen who look as if they might be peasants or mule drivers, dressed in corduroy suits, black sashes, and shirts buttoned up to the top, are patiently waiting for a trout to bite. A little way farther down some women are washing clothes.

The traveler eats some candies and pastry in a shop beside the bridge, and then he smokes a cigarette at the door with some men who have already come back from work. The group gets to be quite large and the traveler mentions that he would like to see the town. Three or four men of about his own age go with him. The taverns in Trillo have a rowdy, cheerful air, as if a commotion were about to break out at any minute. The traveler finds the people friendly and obliging, anxious to make themselves agreeable. He tells this to his friends and one of them answers smiling, "Around here they call us 'the bad people,' so there you are!"

Outside a tavern the group meets a young man. One of the traveler's companions says to him, "I'm going to introduce you to our mayor."

The traveler and the mayor greet each other.

"A pleasure."

"The pleasure's mine."

"So? You're seeing this part of the country on foot?"

"Well, yes . . . just strolling around."

The traveler and the mayor can't find much to say to each other.

"Do you need anything?"

"No, thanks very much."

The mayor of Trillo appears to be thirty years old or so and is a tailor by trade. He also has a shop which sells materials and ready-made goods.

As the group strolls around the town the conversation turns to the subject of the local leprosarium.

"At first we felt a little nervous about this leprosy business, but now we're getting used to it."

An old man breaks in, "The pity is that the baths of Carlos III were abandoned, for they were famous all over Spain. Maybe you remember the proverb, 'Trillo cures all sadness but the

French disease and madness.' "

"But aren't you people afraid you'll catch leprosy?"

The men glance at each other before they answer.

"No, not really. It's one of those things, don't you know, that some folks have and others don't."

Before he goes back to the inn the traveler takes note of some surnames, the surnames of the Alcarria. In all these towns he has been meeting people named Batanero, Gamo, Ochaíta, Bachiller, Arbeteta, Bermejo, Rodrigo, Alvaro, Laina, Romo, Bodega, and Poyatos.

"Some come from one place and some from another, you mustn't assume that they're all mixed together."

"No, of course not."

Back at the inn while he waits for his supper, the traveler reads in the book that Julio Vacas gave him in Brihuega, what it says about the waters of Trillo. Don Ramón Tomé is the translator of the *Practical Treatise on Gout* and the author of the *Treatise on Baths and Fountains of Mineral Waters* which comes at the end of the book. Don Ramón Tomé describes briefly the location of the town—two leagues from Cifuentes, on the banks of the Tajo, in the province of Guadalajara and the diocese of Sigüenza—and cites the testimony of Don Eugenio Antonio Peñafiel, physician of Trillo, already referred to in the account of the waters written by Don Casimiro Ortega, on the curious case of the Baron de Mesnis, first lieutenant of the Royal Walloon Guards, a person who apparently arrived in Trillo entirely crippled, and after several days of taking the waters mixed with goat's-milk whey, began to recover and was able to retire to the Court, filled with satisfaction, according to the chronicler. This occurred in 1768.

When the traveler was called to supper a hundred and sixty-odd years later, he was thinking about how pleased Baron de Mesnis must have felt after his visit to the thermal baths of Trillo.

There were two men in the dining room, traveling salesmen as the traveler found out later, who were having coffee. They had already finished their supper but had decided to wait a while before going to bed. One of them, the older one, was reading a newspaper called *The New Alcarria.* The other, the young one, was writing up his accounts in a notebook. The traveler took his seat before a plate of fried eggs and sausage.

"Good evening."

"Good evening, enjoy the meal."

"Care for some?"

"No thanks, we've already eaten."

The salesmen left off reading and writing, respectively, and glanced at the traveler. Both of them were curious, especially the young one, but at first, to tell the truth, they couldn't make up their minds to speak. The older man gave the impression of being taciturn, gloomy, and preoccupied. The young one, by contrast, was a talkative fellow, short in stature and eager to please, who tried to make himself agreeable. His name was Martín and he was a salesman for a factory which turned out canvas sandals, with hemp or rubber soles as preferred. The traveler found out that the older man traveled from one place to another by bus, and when he couldn't do that, on foot. Martín, however, always went by bicycle and had a sporting outlook on life.

"When my iron steed's in good shape," he told the traveler, "I could go to the ends of the earth to sell sandals."

The traveler hadn't doubted the truth of that statement for an instant.

"To push any article, you've got to put yourself out and have a lot of patience; take a lot of trouble and put up with a lot, because otherwise you don't get anywhere."

"And do you sell nothing but sandals?"

"No indeed, I sell everything there's a use for. So maybe in one town they don't have buttons, or darning cotton, or letter paper? Well, I go there, write a postcard to my firm and pass on to something else. A man wouldn't even make expenses if he only dealt in one article."

One reaches the dining room through the kitchen. When the traveler came in, the woman who keeps the inn was eating there with the help.

"The people in these towns are really foxy, you know?"

As he spoke the salesman was rolling a cigarette with tobacco from the traveler's pouch.

"The minute they catch you napping, they'll trick you every time. But that's not so bad, it keeps you on your toes."

The salesman puffs away on his cigarette and tilts his head to one side. The other man has already folded up his paper and watches in silence.

"Spain's a very ignorant country, there's no culture here, there's a lot of illiteracy. I had three years of secondary school, though you might not think so to see me now. But I don't complain; I'm making a living and I let it go at that. I'll get rich some day if I can, and if I can't—well, look, we can't all be lucky. Right now I try to lead a healthy life and be outdoors, because you know what they used to say in olden times: a healthy mind in a healthy body. I studied with the Salesian Brothers; some of my classmates are doctors now, or construction supervisors, and they live like kings. I don't associate with them because I don't care to; when I do meet them I want to be as good as they are and have a home the way a man ought to, because I'm very proud."

"Yes, that's the truth."

"You bet it is, it's a big fat truth. After all, we're all made of the same stuff."

After making this confession the salesman asks the traveler, as if unwillingly, "And how about you?"

"I? Well, as you see!"

"When they told me there was a new gentleman here, I thought maybe you were from the district judiciary."

"No, thank God, I'm not from the district judiciary."

The salesman is somewhat puzzled.

"Because, I said to myself, you're not a salesman. We would have run across each other somewhere."

"Naturally."

The woman who keeps the inn appears with some bananas for dessert and a cup of coffee, and the traveler asks her about a guide who might be able to take him across the Tetas de Viana; any boy who knows the road and can supply some kind of mount to carry the baggage. The woman thinks for a moment.

"Not unless you'd like to take my Quico."

"And who's your Quico?"

"He's my oldest boy; he's eighteen now."

After making arrangements with the woman, the traveler goes off to bed. Martín goes up with him, for their two beds are in the same room.

"Where are you going from here?"

"Well, I don't know for sure. Maybe I'll go to Budia, maybe to Pareja."

Once they are in bed with the light off, the salesman asks, "Don't you care which place you go to?"

"Well, no, to tell the truth. Why should I?"

A little later, after he has turned over in bed for the last time before shutting his eyes, the salesman tries again. "Listen, pardon my curiosity, but when you eat fried eggs do you always have five?"

The traveler doesn't answer; he pretends to be asleep. Outside, in the midst of an awesome silence, the waterfall of the Cifuentes is roaring monotonously.

7. FROM THE TAJO TO THE STREAM OF SOLEDAD

THE traveler gets up at six. Dawn is just breaking. The traveler has slept well all night through without waking up. He washes, dresses, folds up his blanket, slings his pack on his shoulder and goes out. Martín, who is awake, speaks to him.

"Good morning."

"Good morning, did you sleep well?"

"Fine, and you?"

"Just fine. Aren't you going to get up?"

"No, not yet; since I've got the bicycle . . ."

"Of course."

Quico is at the door with his mule, waiting for the traveler. Quico is a sturdy youngster, very well washed and combed, wearing a clean, absolutely immaculate shirt. Quico's mother has got up to get her son ready and to cook the traveler's breakfast.

Quico's mule is named Jardinera; she is chestnut-colored, young, not very large, and appears to be of good stock.

The traveler and his associates cross the Tajo and start off along a goat track which goes up the hill called La Dehesa. Quico tells the traveler that, so people say, the Americans took away the Monastery of Oliva stone by stone before the Civil War.

On La Dehesa the herbage is harsh and fragrant, composed of hawthorn, rosemary, lavender, sage, marjoram, broom, gorse, spurge flax, spike, rockrose, dwarf oak, and thyme. You can scarcely see it but you get dizzy smelling it. The sun is not very warm yet, though the day promises to be fair. The air is transparent. The Tajo, which seen close to is a muddy, ugly river, seems from a distance to be beautiful and very elegant. It winds as it goes and you can see it a long way off, always with trees on either side. The leprosarium is visible on its banks, in the foreground. It is made up of several large buildings and a few smaller houses. Quico explains to the traveler the buildings they are looking at; this is such-and-such, that is something else, and over there is another thing. Then he smiles and says, with a sorrowful look, "Miserable people, aren't they?"

"Yes."

"Those poor folks haven't had much luck, have they?"

"That's right."

At the traveler's feet, on the near side of the river, goes the highway to Azañón and Peralveche.

"You can go to Viana and La Puerta that way too."

"And this way."

"Oh, yes, this way too. There's a shortcut near here that goes straight to Viana."

The traveler wants to take advantage of the coolness and also of the fact that the mule is carrying his pack, and he walks straight on without stopping, or stopping for only a few seconds now and then to look at the landscape.

Going through the Entrepeña, the traveler sees a beautiful stage setting, exactly as if it were in a theater, of great craggy naked rocks and dead trees split by lightning. A bird of prey is hovering with a young rabbit in its talons. An immense green, yellow, and red lizard scurries right out from under the traveler's feet.

As they come out on the stretch of land called Fuente de la Galinda, the Tetas de Viana suddenly thrust themselves into view. The Fuente de la Galinda is a low stony slope with a great deal of game on it. A flock of partridge flies straight up, slowly and in plain sight as if unused to hunters, only a few steps away from the group.

Quico and the traveler call the first halt, take a drink, smoke a cigarette, and have a chat.

"They killed a man right here once."

The traveler thinks to himself that the place was very well chosen; it certainly is an appropriate spot.

"Really?"

"Yes, señor. First they shot him with slugs and then they knifed him twenty times anyway."

"They must have left him in fine shape!"

"Yes, señor, they left him dead. The man that got killed was from Sotoca."

"And who killed him?"

"Nobody knows that; how could anybody know!"

A nest of wasps is buzzing in the hollow of a tree.

"They stole the dead man's money and cut off his ears."

"Not bad!"

"Well, I don't know about that, it depends on how you look at it. It used to be the custom, they say."

"And how about now?"

"No, I think nowadays things like that don't happen so often."

Beyond the Fuente de la Galinda one crosses the hills called Las Acacias, some low slopes which fall away to the plain of El Olivar Hueco. On the lower slopes of the Tetas de Viana there are a few meadows of tender green grass, surrounded by brambles and thorn bushes.

"The shortcut goes all along here, to the left. To get up to the Tetas you have to get off the path. The farther one has a wooden ladder right up to the top of it; it was an observation post during the war. Do you want to climb up there?"

"No, we're fine where we are."

The two Tetas are almost exactly alike seen from the north, with the more westerly one a little higher perhaps. They have the shape of a cone with its tip cut off and each one has a flat top with rocky, sheer edges which must be difficult to scale.

As they reach the top of the slope the traveler discovers a view which is beautiful in the foreground but which farther off seems a little desolate. A few paths, some of them almost completely obliterated, begin to branch off from the main one. The mule walks cautiously, taking a great deal of care, and the stones roll under her feet at times.

Halfway down the mountainside is the fountain of El Pilón. The traveler would have liked to freshen up a bit. The heat is already very oppressive, and Quico and the traveler feel great drops of sweat rolling down their faces as they walk.

"Shall we wash up a little?"

"Wait a minute, the fountain of San Juan is down there and it's better."

And indeed, shortly afterward the fountain of San Juan appears in a bend of the path, hidden among trees. The traveler refreshes himself, stripping to the waist and then putting himself out to dry in the sun. Quico has moistened only his arms and his forehead.

"Water's very treacherous, you know; sometimes you catch something you didn't have before."

The Tetas are much uglier seen from the south; they look ungainly, malformed, crooked, as it were.

The mule, rid of the baggage, is cropping the ferns around the fountain. A group of six or seven turkey-bustards go over, flying very high. The frogs are croaking and the lizards peer covertly from the hollows of the rocks, stare for a moment, and then scurry away.

The traveler descends a ravine and arrives at Viana de Mondéjar, a yellow-colored town laid out on a blunt blackish hill.

The traveler doesn't go into Viana; he stays just outside, lunching with Quico in the shade of a little bunch of squalid poplar trees on the banks of the Solana, a wretched little river with almost no water in it, which drags its insufficiency down from the Sierra de Umbría Seca.

After lunch the traveler, who has returned to more level ground, dismisses Quico and his mule Jardinera, lies down in the shade, and pulls his hat over his eyes. In a short time he is deeply asleep, a gentle, cool, comforting sleep.

When he wakes up he gets to his feet, stretches a bit, slings on his pack, and sets off. Some time must have passed, for Quico and his mule Jardinera are already on the other side of the Tetas; they are nowhere to be seen.

A woman is silently washing clothes, bareheaded under a blazing sun. It is noon. The silence is complete and the only thing to be heard is the faint noise of the Solana with an incessant croaking serving as a background to it.

As far as La Puerta the road goes along the banks, or very close to the banks, of the stream; sometimes it wanders away and then garden plots begin to appear between the stream and the road. To get into the town one crosses a small, graceful stone bridge. The Solana passes beneath it and then glides on between two great masses of rock in the shape of a saw, or better still, of a cock's comb. The name of the town, The Gateway, is perfectly explicable.

The traveler goes into the town and searches out the inn. But there they have nothing for him to eat. He asks at a few houses in the town and they all tell him the same thing. The traveler, who was somewhat tired already, becomes quite exhausted from walking up and down the town. The mayor says that he can give him a loaf of bread at least.

"We're poor, as you can see, but nobody who ever passed through La Puerta has gone away without some bread. Did they tell you at the lodging house that there wasn't anything?"

"Yes, they did."

"It isn't really a lodging house any more, understand? Once in a while they have somebody but it isn't a real one any more."

The mayor and the traveler go to the town hall, which is a dilapidated stable with a little office in one corner. The men of the town are gathered in the hall, sitting on the floor or leaning against the chipped walls. When the mayor arrives they stand up and take off their caps; when he sits down they sit down too and put them on again. When one of them speaks he does so standing up, touching his hand to his cap.

The mayor is a tall, broad-shouldered man of about forty. The inhabitants of La Puerta live from making charcoal and from what they grow in their gardens; they do a little fishing as well. The traveler observes that almost all of them have blue eyes. The people round about call them "Fat-calves":

The folk of La Puerta
All have fat calves;

Seven pairs of stockings
Some of them have.

The traveler comes to the conclusion, while the men of La Puerta are talking of their affairs, that the best thing to do would be to rest for a few hours and then go on to somewhere else. When they have finished, the traveler talks with the mayor.

"The trouble is that Budia's quite a distance away."

"That doesn't matter. I'd be glad to pay for a cart if someone feels like taking me."

The traveler returns to the inn to sleep a few hours if he can. The mayor had agreed to send the cart at six or seven in the evening, when the men begin to come in from the fields.

The traveler pokes his nose into the kitchen. His pack is almost empty; only a hard-boiled egg and two oranges are left. The woman of the house offers him a few chunks of cooked goat's meat and a glass of milk, also goat's. The traveler thinks about Malta fever and then about the saying that the horn of hunger gores deepest of all, and eats everything she gives him; the meat is dry and hard and all but unchewable, and the milk has a harsh, wild, sweetish taste. As the traveler eats he is surrounded by a group of three or four skinny, mournful dogs and an equal number of wary, wild-eyed cats who don't come close enough to be touched and who snarl and bite at each other constantly. In one corner of the kitchen is an earthen jar for making lye. Great heavy dippers and copper pots decorate the walls. In one corner is an advertisement for corduroy cloth superimposed on the colors of the flag and a "Viva España!" Crouching in front of the fireplace preparing some food is a young and very beautiful woman with a little girl, not a baby any more, really, in her arms. The little girl's name is Rosita.

The woman of the house has sat down on a low wooden stool and is talking with the traveler.

"Are you a traveling salesman?"

"No, señora."

"Are you one of those actors, maybe?"

The traveler makes a few funny faces and the women begin to laugh. He keeps on and the women are soon screaming with laughter, slapping their thighs and saying, "Stop it, stop it!" The traveler gets up and takes two hops over the kneading trough, pretending to be lame. The women are crimson, choking, convulsed with laughter. The traveler couldn't help laughing either, when he squatted on the bench scratching his head like a monkey. Little Rosita has started to cry. The cats have fled in terror and the dogs are barking from the entrance way.

"No, señora, I'm not an actor either."

"Well, you could certainly earn yourself a good living making those faces."

"Yes, maybe so."

The traveler finishes his meal and lies down to take a siesta in an immense, irregularly-shaped room, on a bed with five straw mattresses on it and as big as a bullring. In the bedroom are five or six tin trunks of different colors, raised off the floor on blocks and covered with flowered spreads of orange and blue. There are also an unpainted wooden table without the usual cloth to conceal its nakedness, two gilt-framed mirrors, and a host of colored advertisements and photographs of a bearded lieutenant of the Spanish-American War. The pictures on the advertisements are extremely varied: a sultan in a turban with an emerald in the center advertises a brand of coffee; a swarthy gypsy girl with deep dreamy eyes, some superphosphate fertilizers; a dove flying over the roofs of a city, a grocery in Madrid: "Fine Products of the Realm and Overseas." The finishing touch to these adornments is a map of Europe of the time of the Austro-Hungarian Empire, with little flags of all the nations painted around the edges, and those of France and Spain in the center forming a loop, above an ornamental wreath which reads "Liberté, Egalité, Fraternité" and the legend "Visitez le Maroc."

The traveler takes off his shoes, leaning on a high-backed armchair that resembles a throne. Beside it is a washstand as skinny as a spider, with the basin full of long, sweet-smelling, silky woman's hair. After noticing this, the traveler discovers that the high-backed chair is used as a barber's chair. On a lined sheet of paper fastened to the wall with four tacks, the traveler reads a notice written in ink in very carefully formed handwriting: "La

Puerta Barbershop. Price of each item. Shave, .75 pesetas. Haircut, plain, .75. Ditto, combed back or parted, 1.00. Ditto, Parisian style, 1.50. With brilliantine, .25. Massage, cologne, .50. Ladies' haircuts, 1.00. La Puerta, January 1, 1945. In charge, Pablo Balcón. Permanent barbering service from 11:00 A.M. to 11:00 P.M. Closed Thursdays."

The traveler takes a jump onto the bed, covers himself up, and soon goes to sleep, not before having observed the stone floor, the heavy chestnut beams in the ceiling, and the massive nail-studded wooden door.

At six o'clock the traveler gets up, washes in the entrance way in a deep pail of very cool water which the woman of the house had brought him, dresses, and goes out. In front of the doorway are the mayor and the man with the mule cart whom he has found. The mayor of La Puerta has his finger on everything; not the least detail escapes him; he is a shining example of a mayor; he and the mayor of Pastrana, whom the traveler is to meet several days later, are the two best mayors in the Alcarria.

The traveler settles the details of the trip before he tosses his pack into the cart.

"It seems a little expensive."

The cart driver had asked a hundred pesetas.

"But just consider that I'll have to sleep in Budia; at the hour we'll get there I'll be in no shape to start back. I don't want to be so sleepy I'll roll all the way home."

"Even so!"

The mayor intervenes and the man comes down by degrees to sixty pesetas.

The traveler departs from La Puerta along the valley of the stream named Acorbaíllo. He is reclining almost full-length in the cart, protecting himself from the sun under a blanket which serves as an awning and which nearly smothers him with its heat. As they go along, the traveler talks with the cart driver, who is sitting up with his legs outside. The mule is a plow mule; you can see he's not used to a cart, for he gets into the ditch as soon as the man's attention wanders, and kicks when the whip touches him.

"In Budia you'll find anything you want; all these towns are very poor, around here there's only enough for the ones of us who live in them, and don't think there's much left over either. Budia is a really rich town; there everybody, high and low, has money to spend."

"How about Cereceda?"

"Cereceda is very poor too, like us. It's over there behind those hills."

After leaving La Puerta the road goes with the river Solana on its left; at the level of Cereceda, which lies behind a peak called El Tornero, there is a little bridge to cross and then the river runs parallel to the road until it flows into the Tajo. Mantiel lies off to the south about a league's distance from Cereceda, with Chillarón del Rey another league away, and Alique and Hontanillas some two leagues, all reached only by mule paths. The traveler, who is following the gorge of the Solana, doesn't see any of these towns. While he is having a smoke with the cart driver he learns that Cereceda people are called "Fat-Calves" like those from La Puerta; those from Mantiel, "Misers" and "Itchies"; from Chillarón, "Mangies"; from Alique, "Tricksters"; and from Hontanillas, "Trough-eaters," because they eat from the pig's trough so as not to get the plates dirty.

It occurs to the traveler that with his pack empty, it would be more prudent not to go up into the hills to search out such towns as these.

"What about people from Budia?"

"They don't have any special name; we just call them "Budieros."

Along the edge of the road there are blackberry bushes, hawthorn thickets, and blossoming wild fig trees. Now the hill of Aleja appears to the south and the stretch of land called La Nava to the north. A little later comes the crossing of the Tajo and the road runs beside it for half an hour. After that there is a branch road which turns off from the highway and goes to Durón and Budia and reaches Brihuega; and even, still farther on, joins the national highway to Zaragoza. The road which continues along the banks of the Tajo goes to Sacedón, with a branch road to

Pareja on the banks of the Empolveda.

The traveler has climbed down from the cart to stretch his legs for a while. As they go past Durón, which is on the left and a little off the road, it is beginning to get dark. There is a small group of houses on the highway. Some men and women and a whole swarm of children are resting in the doorways. Going through the cut of El Tirador—a very narrow gorge between two mountains, Trascastillo on the left and Castillo de Maraña on the right—the traveler's journey is enlivened by four or five flashes of lightning, one right after the other, which light up the mountains and crackle in his ears like so many whiplashes. The thunder rumbles and then comes a gust of warm air so strong that the traveler and the cart driver have to hold on to the cart to keep it from turning over. The mule, whose name is Morico, gets frightened, whinnies, kicks out in all directions, and rears back. His owner subdues him with blows and insults. It begins to rain in torrents and the two men take shelter under the cart, which they have pulled off into the ditch, and bundle up in their blankets.

When it clears up a little, the night is already pitch-dark. The sky is clear and cloudless. The mule is soaking wet, shiny in the moonlight as if he had been dipped in oil. He seems placid and rested too, as though refreshed by the rain.

The traveler doesn't reach Budia until midnight. He goes into the plaza and they look at him as if he were a rare bird indeed. Budia is a town where the people don't go to bed early, where the young men stay in the taverns playing dominoes and never worry about how late it is.

The traveler goes into the inn with the mule's owner behind him. The traveler has invited his companion to have supper with him, but the companion refuses.

"Don't bother, I brought something with me."

The man takes the mule to the stable, gives him a pail of water and an armful of feed, takes his lunch out of a bag, eats it, and lies down in the entryway wrapped in his damp blanket to wait till morning.

The traveler has little success at the inn.

"Can I get anything to eat?"

"There isn't a thing, unless you go and buy it!"

The traveler reflects that at this hour of the night he isn't going to find much of anything.

"All right. I'll try to find some eggs and milk."

The woman of the house looks him over from top to bottom. Apparently she doesn't like the look of him, for she says, "I can't fix anything for you; this isn't really a lodging house any more."

The traveler goes off with his tail between his legs, feeling dejected; he is thinking about the Mayor of Cork.* At the door he bumps into Martín, the salesman he had made friends with in Trillo.

"I thought you might wind up here, but it seemed pretty late in the day for it."

"Well, here I am. Listen, do you know anyone who might fix me up with some supper, even though it doesn't amount to much?"

"Don't give it a thought; come along with me."

Martín, who is a man who can do anything, takes the traveler to a tavern, talks to the owner's wife, and returns with a victor's smile.

"All set. I'll stay with you while you have your supper."

While the table is being set, Martín, who apparently had found out more in Trillo than the traveler had imagined, explains to a young fellow in a bow tie who the newcomer is. The young fellow listens carefully and nods his head in agreement; then he turns to the traveler and says, "I know what you're doing, it's that book with a blue binding and a shield on the front, that lists all the mayors and all the business people in the province. It's not a bad idea at all, it really isn't!"

The traveler acknowledges the young man's polite remarks with a smile.

After supper the traveler invites Martín to a drink. Martín has anisette and the traveler has cognac.

They go back to the inn and at the door Martín says, "Don't

*Terence McSwiney, Lord Mayor of Cork, arrested by the British on charges of sedition, died on October 25, 1920, after fasting for 74 days. [Translator's note.]

you say a word, now."

"All right."

Martín talks to the woman of the house and she glances in the traveler's direction. She goes out of the room, returns a short while later, and says, "Your bed's ready. This girl here will show you."

Lying in bed, the traveler can hardly believe in so much good fortune. He has a smoke, turns off the light, settles himself in bed and closes his eyes to sleep.

From the other bed Martín's voice was saying. "If you go to Campo de Criptana, ask for Herrerillo, tell him you come from me, Martín, the one who used to be in Military Government headquarters in Madrid; he'll know."

The room is almost hermetically closed; it is like a box, with no ventilation at all, not even a skylight, and the traveler doesn't wake up till ten in the morning. Martín is already up, but he comes back after a little while.

"I've been coming up once in a while to see if you were awake yet. I've been around town doing my little bits of business."

Martín stops for breath.

"Well, had a good rest?"

"Man, I should say I have! I feel like a new person. Last night I was feeling a little fed-up."

"So, what's the use of thinking about it? It's all over now!"

There is no doubt that Martín is a stoic.

The traveler goes out with Martín and takes a walk around the town. The plaza looks as though it could be in an Arab town; the façade of the town hall is whitewashed and has a gallery with graceful arches in the upper part of it. Eight or ten mules with no harness come trotting into the plaza, driven by a tall young man in a black blouse; they take a long drink in the trough and then roll in the dust with all four feet in the air. An old man is sitting in the sun under the colonnades.

Budia is a large town with old houses, and probably has had a splendid past. The streets have noble and sonorous names—Royal, Wineskin Merchants', Street of the Steppe, of the Gable, of Bronze, of Lettuce, of the Hospital—and in the streets the expiring palaces bear with a kind of dignity their carved family crests, their massive doors, and their great, sad, closed-up windows.

The traveler goes round to the doctor's house to pay him a visit. The doctor lives on the plaza in a two-story house which is clean and neat, with good furniture and French engravings on the walls. The doctor in Budia is the father of one of the traveler's friends. There is a piano in the front hall of the house. A maid, still young, dressed in mourning, opens the door for him.

"I'll go call the doctor; he'll be glad to have you bring him news of Mr. Alfredo."

The doctor is not long in appearing. His name is Don Severino and he is a charming, talkative, jovial old fellow; he takes the traveler inside and invites him to some biscuits and sherry, the biscuits from a deep canister which seems inexhaustible, the sherry a whole bottle.

"If we finish up these, we'll ask for more."

The doctor and the traveler talk about the town. The doctor has published a book with the title, *Data for a Medico-topographical Study of the City of Budia, by Don Severino Domínguez Alonso, Physician by Appointment of the Same.* The book was printed in Guadalajara in 1907, at the printing press of Antero Concha, Plaza San Esteban (Post Office Square), Number 2.

The traveler leafs through the book and discovers that Budia lies along the sides of a hill called Cuesta Cabeza and that the so-called Communal Lands are used for grazing and firewood. Budia is a town which has a great deal of water, though not as much as Cifuentes. The water of the fountain of Tobilla is used to combat affections of the stomach; for drinking, the New Fountain is used; and for cooking vegetables, the one near the stream of Soledad. The spring of El Cuerno, though it is the best of all, is used for irrigation of the fields, since it is difficult to canalize and it would be too expensive to do so.

Don Severino offers the traveler some good Havana tobacco.

"The stomach is the barometer of health."

"Of course."

"Formerly the migrant laborers used to go out once a year and come back well-nourished, with a hundred pesetas apiece. In those days," adds Don Severino with a nostalgic wave of his hand, "they used to eat very well indeed."

The traveler feels charmed; the sherry, the biscuits, and the tobacco have agreed with him marvelously.

"The natives here take their brandy on an empty stomach; they say it serves to kill pinworms."

A big black cat with shining fur slips through the open window of the dining room.

"They're apt to use coffee as a medicine."

The traveler, sitting at Don Severino's table, feels as though he could spend the rest of his life there.

"There are more than seven hundred different aromatic herbs around here; maybe that's why the honey is of such good quality."

"Naturally . . ."

A dangerous drowsiness floods in upon the traveler. He is entirely too comfortable in the doctor's rocking chair. Toward noon he goes out on the street again, anxious to take to the country at once. The sunlight is falling directly on the plaza; the only shadows to be seen are the very small ones under the eaves of the roofs. An old woman seated on a low chair is knitting in the sun, while a very small child is playing in the dirt beside her.

An idiot beggar boy with only one eye is passing through the plaza. He walks rigidly, ceremonially, slowly, and around him are a couple of dozen boys who are staring at him in silence. The idiot has a wound in his head which is still bleeding, and everything about him gives an impression of profound and extraordinary sadness. He drags his feet along, leaning on a sort of crook, with his back bent over and his chest sunken. In a grating, cracked, spine-chilling voice the idiot is singing:

"Jesus my Saviour,
Jesus my love,
Open your heart to me
From Heaven above."

A woman carrying a child appears in a doorway.

"Too bad you didn't kick the bucket long ago, you scum!"

8. FROM THE STREAM OF SOLEDAD TO THAT OF EMPOLVEDA

THE traveler leaves Budia before lunchtime, going along the banks of the Lapelos, which later runs into the Tajo. He had thought he would return to Durón by the same road along which he had come to Budia, but changes his mind and goes right up the mountainside, sometimes taking paths that are almost obliterated, to get near El Olivar. Then he'll go down to Durón again and take the highway.

El Olivar is about half a league from Budia and somewhat higher up. It is a poverty-stricken town lost among the mountains, in a countryside haunted by wolves and surrounded by gullies.

A shepherd is watching his flock in the gorge of a stream. He is a surly, weatherbeaten man of about fifty, who speaks little at first and then begins to warm up. His name is Roque and he has just clubbed a marten to death, a marten which he shows the traveler.

"What'll you give me?"

"You set the price."

"No, I won't do that."

The man throws the marten away.

"You'll give me something all right, if you want it."

"How about ten pesetas?"

The shepherd opens his eyes wide with astonishment.

"Hand them over!"

The traveler takes the ten pesetas out of his pocket, gives them to the shepherd, and touches the marten with his toe.

"Now it's mine."

"Wait'll I skin it. If you leave it that way, it'll smell pretty quick."

The shepherd whisks off the skin in no time, with great skill. Then he sticks his knife into the raw flesh of the breast three or four times and tosses the carcass to the dogs, who devour it greedily, growling all the while.

The traveler, who has replenished his supplies in Budia, opens his pack to eat.

"Is this water good to drink?"

"Well, it hasn't killed me yet."

The traveler opens a can of tuna and offers it to the shepherd.

"I already ate."

"That doesn't matter."

"All right, then."

The shepherd eats it all and then drinks the oil out of the can. The traveler opens another can; it was a mistake to think that one was going to be enough for the two of them. Among other things, it says on the can, "Net weight, 750 grams." Then he drinks a bowl of milk which the shepherd gives him.

"There's always some ewe whose lamb has died who keeps us in milk."

At the top of the gorge is a ledge from which the Tajo can be seen. The traveler climbs up to it with the shepherd, while the sheep stay with the dogs.

"Rest easy, none of them will get lost. The main thing about managing them is to have a good sheepdog."

During the climb the shepherd and the traveler swap a piece of dried meat for two oranges. Then they both have a swig out of the canteen.

"Lovely view."

"Yes, so they say. Listen, are you from Guadalajara, maybe?"

"No, why?"

"Nothing; it's just that everybody from Guadalajara says the same thing when they come up here."

The traveler pretends he hasn't heard and begins to talk

about how good the land must be, down there on the river bank.

"Yes, señor, it certainly is! That land is really good; around here, you know, the poor part is up in the hills; as you go down toward the flat part you begin to find good easy land, very favorable it is."

"Do they do a good job of cultivating it?"

"Sure they do, as good as any place, if not better."

The traveler, as he descends the slope talking and smoking with the shepherd, sees some distance away a wild-looking boy with his hair grown down over his neck and his chest bare. The boy is standing stock-still on a rock a hundred paces away. The traveler calls to him and the boy neither moves nor answers. The shepherd advises the traveler to leave him alone.

"Don't pay any attention to him, I know him well. That one's a kid from El Olivar, his name is Saturnino. He's always roaming around here trying to see what he can pick up. He's an artful kid, and cunning; a real tricky one. Last year I all but knocked him down with a rock. I had two sucking lambs missing and I always thought he was the one that took them."

"Is he always up here in the hills?"

"Yes, señor, always; he's just like a marten, he's even got a hide like a marten. But what I say is, they'll tame him in the army. If he's signed up, that is; for all I know that one's not even on the lists."

Back with the flock again, the traveler says goodbye to his friend Roque and starts out in search of Durón. You can't see the town till you're right on top of it. The traveler has gone a little out of the way and reaches the town by way of the mountain of Trascastillo; on its lower slope is the cut of El Tirador which he crossed yesterday after nightfall on his way to Budia. The slope of Trascastillo is very steep, almost sheer; at one point it looks as though one would be able to get over to the other mountain, Castillo de Maraña, in a single leap. The traveler has to take the descent very carefully so as not to slip and break his ribs, and about halfway along he sits down to rest for a while. Through the cut of El Tirador and beside the highway runs the Soledad, with some little meadows along its banks almost hidden in the trees; it is a very bucolic landscape, which looks as if it had been taken from a tapestry.

Durón is a town in three sections, two on the side of the mountain and a smaller one along the road the traveler is about to take, beside the garden plots.

At the doors of the houses the traveler sees the same group of men and women, the same swarm of noisy children as the day before. Durón is a town where the people are open and pleasant and treat a passerby kindly; they are curious and even friendly with the traveler. It is amusing to notice how different, even at this short distance, the people of Budia are from those of Durón; in Durón they talk and laugh and show a favorable attitude.

"If you get as far as Pareja be sure to go up to Casasana, it's my home town."

The speaker is a young woman, the mother of a child some two years old, who keeps climbing up on a cart which is lying in the ditch; he falls off, cries a little, climbs up again, falls off again, cries another little while, and, as they tell the traveler, spends the whole afternoon doing this. Now and again the mother gives him a spank on the bottom and then the youngster cries a little harder for a few minutes, wanders squalling among the crowd and then, naturally, climbs right up on the cart again.

"My mother's the one who keeps the lodging house, tell her you've seen me and that I'm fine, we're all fine. My brother's on the town council in Casasana and his name is Fabián, Fabián Gabarda. Write it down so you won't forget."

Four or five black poplars as thin as whistles are swaying in the afternoon breeze.

An old man with most of his teeth missing talks to the traveler; he wears glasses and a beret, carries a stick, has a six-day beard, and has his corduroy jacket slung over his shoulder bullfighter style.

"So, young man, you live in Madrid?"

"Yes, señor."

"D'you know Ramiro, the one who works in the eye clinic?"

"No, señor."

"And Julián?"

"No, I don't know Julián either."

The old man in glasses looks at the traveler suspiciously, as if to say, "No; this one's not from Madrid, God knows where he's come from! If he were really from Madrid he'd know Ramiro and Julián. Everybody knows who they are."

The old man looks at the ground and taps the stones with his stick a few times. Then he raises his head again and speaks.

"The year the war was over I was in Madrid, I went to have an operation for cataracts. My son Paco went with me, I couldn't manage by myself. He's out in the fields right now, if you wait a while you can meet him, I don't think he'll be long now. I don't go out to the fields any more, I'm not good for it any longer. I went out for forty years, never missed a day till I had to call it quits."

The old man smiles. "Time catches up with us all, as you see. When I got so I was no good, my son Paco wasn't quite twelve years old. I gave him the tools and I said, 'Here's your gear, you know where the field is.' He's a good son, and since then he's carried all the weight. You see, there's just the two of us; the mother died when the boy was born. It's better for Paquito to be here working his own land; at least, that's what I think."

The traveler drinks a bowl of sheep's milk which one of the women has offered him. Then he says goodbye and starts off. Roads are made for walking on, and it gets to be a bad habit to sit by the roadside talking to people.

A short time after leaving Durón, before the junction with the Tajo, night overtakes the traveler. The darkness comes on rapidly, almost precipitately. At the junction a pair of civil guardsmen request his papers.

"What are you doing out on the road at this hour?"

"I meant to get as far as Pareja."

"To Pareja? You'll be walking all night, it's more than three leagues from here, nearer four. But that's your affair! Your documents are in order."

The traveler and the civil guardsmen walk on together for an hour, as far as the bridge.

"We're staying here. You go straight on to Pareja. Turn right at the first crossroads, go left at the second."

"Many thanks."

"Don't mention it."

The three men sit down to have a smoke. The guards are pleasant fellows. One is old and moustached, resembling a guardsman of the early part of the century; he tells filthy jokes which are hoary with age. The other one is young and almost delicate-looking; he is circumspect, serious and silent. In the moonlight the group probably looks strange and ghostly.

"Am I bothering you, Torremocha? If I am, I'll shut up."

There is a slight touch of irony in the words of the moustached guardsman.

"No, Señor Pérez, go ahead."

Señor Pérez feels himself obliged to explain.

"My friend Torremocha here, see, changed his tastes in the Glorious National Movement. He traded the service of the saints for the service of arms, and as far as I'm concerned he fell between two stools."

Guardsman Torremocha says nothing, but his silence carries no note of agreement.

"Did you used to read that comic magazine *Many Thanks*?"

"Sometimes."

"Say, what a magazine! Those birds were really killing, the things they used to think of! And the *Chronicle*?"

"Once in a while, too."

"I was posted to Carabanchel Barracks in those days, and every time I got the chance, wham! off to Madrid to the burlesque shows at the Eslava or the Martín. Now I'm just an old hulk!"

Guardsman Pérez smoothes his moustache and puffs on his cigarette. With his carbine in its sling, asking for travelers' identity cards along the roads of the Alcarria, Guardsman Pérez is a man who lives off his memories.

A kilometer or two farther on, at the crossroads which goes to Chillarón del Rey, the traveler unfolds his blanket and lies down to sleep at the edge of the highway, under a hawthorn bush. The night is calm and starry. An owl is hooting from an olive tree and a cricket sings among the thistles. The traveler, who is tired, is soon sleeping quietly, deeply, refreshingly . . .

It is still dark when he wakes up; he takes a swallow of wine, eats two oranges and a hunk of bread, and starts walking more vigorously than ever, never feeling the pack or his legs on the road.

The first faint light of dawn finds him already in sight of Pareja, in a region of rich, well-cultivated fields of reddish clay, full of small plots among which he can see an occasional brick-yard with the people already hard at work.

Pareja is a big busy town, with new houses beside others in ruins and an inn on the town plaza. The plaza is square and roomy; in the center is a fountain with a number of spouts and a basin all around, and an ancient, heavy-branched patriarchal elm tree, an elm as old perhaps as the oldest building in the town. Standing around the fountain, the women are waiting to fill their pitchers and jars. The women carry their pitchers on their hips and have a hollow reed over their shoulders; they use the reed to guide the water as it falls from the fountain, a couple of yards above the rim of the basin. The women of Pareja show rare skill in hunting down—or rather, in fishing for —the water without spilling a drop.

The traveler enters the inn; he wants to have a hot breakfast, wash up, and then sit down for a little rest. The inn has some tempting rocking chairs and there are two rosy, plump, friendly girls who giggle as they bustle from one place to another carrying crockery, emptying a chamber pot, dusting the furniture, making a bed, scrubbing the floor; all at once, all in glorious confusion, all as merrily as can be. One of the girls is named Elena and the other María. As the traveler watches Elena and María working, he observes that he is being invaded by a lazy, cheerful feeling. The breakfast is really very good. The sparrows are chattering in the old elm on the plaza, opposite the open balcony full of geraniums in pots, and a yellow canary sings in his cage, ruffling his neck feathers. Inside, a cat is sleeping in the sun on the corner of the esparto-grass mat, and a little boy is pissing gloriously, challengingly, off the balcony.

Through the open door of a neighboring room the traveler can see a rachitic, twitching youngster, an epileptic boy who is probably not quite right in the head; he is sitting in a low chair with his unmanageable legs wrapped in a blanket. The traveler feels suddenly overcome with remorse.

In a cloud of dust and a crowd of children, a rickety, noisy, bouncing bus arrives in the plaza; it stops for a few minutes for the people to get off and then takes the road to Escamilla, making a horrendous noise. Some time later, when the bus must be quite a distance away, it can still be heard limping along, whenever the sparrows in the plaza stop their racket for an instant.

Into the plaza comes an old man ringing a bell. The people gather around him and the old man climbs up on some stone slabs. In his left hand he is carrying some bits of paper and with his right he waves and gesticulates like a political agitator. The traveler, who is very comfortable in his rocking chair, doesn't want to bother to get up and listen; he contents himself with occasionally catching on the wing some of what the old man is saying. The rachitic boy, who must be terribly weary of his chair, can't get up to listen; since he can't do anything about it he has to put up with it, and looks toward the plaza with an expression of envy, stupid and animal-like.

The old man, who is wearing a green velvet beret and has a little white beard, is crying his wares. He has a voice like a cat's or a woman's and positively shrieks to make himself heard. He is small and stooped and looks as though he might be a Jew. The traveler hears bits and pieces of the peddler's spiel.

"The prayer of the Virgin of Carmen and 'The Tomb, or What Love Can Accomplish!' The beautiful tango of Brigadier Villacampa, and the songs of La Parrala and La Pelona! The verses composed by a criminal in the death house in the city of Seville, named Vicente Pérez, a bugler of Havana! 'My Love is Reborn With the News of Your Return!,' the latest creation of Celia Gámez. The atrocities committed by Margarita Cisneros, a young woman of Tamarite! Five céntimos each! Buy the latest popular songs, five céntimos!"

The abnormal boy makes signs to the traveler to make him pay attention. The traveler says, "What do you want?" but he can't understand as well as he would like to because the youngster can hardly talk.

When he comes close to the chair the boy asks him, stammeringly and imperfectly, "Listen, is that man from around here?"

"No, my boy, he's not from here, he's from Priego."

"I thought so; I hadn't ever seen him before."

A stork passes over the elm, flying low.

"Say, give me a cigarette?"

"Take one."

"Listen, if my sisters come and see the smoke, you say it's you, eh?"

"All right."

The stork, carrying a water snake in its bill, disappears over the tops of the houses.

Pareja is a town where the people are full of ideas. A rich farmer, two or three years back, planted beans instead of barley. He issued a proclamation announcing that he would pay twenty céntimos per tap to anyone who wanted to work for him planting beans. The tap in these parts means the hole and each furrow has six of them. He also offered to pay for weeding, one céntimo for every stroke of the hoe. When he settled up accounts after the harvest, he found that he had spent thirty thousand pesetas and had produced beans to the value of one thousand.

The stork flew over the elm again in the opposite direction.

At lunchtime the traveler ate hungrily and abundantly. Elena and María were good little housewives. The traveler had garlic soup and two poached eggs, fried fish (which was not very fresh), and leg of lamb with a tomato-and-lettuce salad.

Afterward the traveler chats for a while with Elena and María. Elena and María are two hardworking, decent girls, healthy in body and soul, accommodating, smiling and very pretty, as are all the women in Pareja. Elena and María would undoubtedly be a good match for any man. Elena loves to cook and María loves children. Elena likes dark men and María likes fair ones. Elena likes the dances on the plaza and María likes walks in the meadow, Elena likes dogs and María likes cats. Elena likes roast lamb and María likes French omelet. Elena likes coffee and María doesn't. Elena likes the High Mass and María doesn't. Elena likes to read the paper and María doesn't. María would rather read the kind of novel in which a country girl, very beautiful of course, marries a young and handsome duke, and they have many children and live happily ever after, with hearth fires in winter and the balconies wide open in summer.

As the traveler listens to Elena and María talking, his thoughts dwell tenderly on polygamy. The temperature is ideal and his stomach is full of noble, ancient victuals, of morsels as historic and traditional as battlefields. If it weren't for the fact that he had promised himself—and really there is no good reason why he should change horses in midstream—not to sleep in the same place for two nights in a row, the traveler would have pitched his camp in Pareja, at the inn on the plaza, and wouldn't have budged from there all the days of his life.

Sometimes one has frightening sensations of well-being, strong enough to move mountains; one must fight against them courageously, as one would fight an enemy. And then, with the passage of time, they leave something like a drop of gall in one's heart . . .

Basking in such felicity, the traveler goes to sleep in the rocker. Elena and María, who are very sensible, have left him alone; but the traveler, between dreaming and waking, half hears them talking—Elena with her little-boy's voice, María with her little-girl's voice—about their enthusiasms, their little worries, about how expensive everything is getting.

When he wakes up, the sun has already set and the first shadows are falling on the elm in the plaza. The traveler must have slept for many hours. He feels a slight chill, gets up and closes the balcony door. Then he sits down again and smokes a cigarette. Nobody comes and the room is almost in darkness. He goes out to the hall and claps his hands twice; the kitchen door opens, lighting up the whole stairwell, and a voice says, "Coming!" The one who spoke was Elena; María is the one who appears.

"Did you call?"

"Yes, my dear. Where's the light switch?"

"It's right there, but wait a minute; we don't have a bulb for that room."

The traveler makes no remark and neither does María. María had said that they had no bulb for that room with tremendous sadness and even with a little quaver in her voice. The traveler smiles. María goes back to the kitchen. The traveler can't make up his mind for a few moments. When he reaches the kitchen he finds María in floods of tears, sitting on a low stool beside the fire. Elena, who is peeling an onion, gives the traveler a ferocious, unexpected glare. Her eyes are bright as if with fever and her chest is heaving.

"What did you say to my sister?"

Her voice, so attractively husky before, now has a horrid metallic ring.

"I—"

Elena interrupts, not letting him finish. "You take your pack and get out. For Heaven's sake! You owe me fourteen pesetas."

The traveler, feeling dejected, went and slept in a tile works on the banks of the Empolveda. A man lived there by himself, a man who wasted no time on the amenities.

"Have you come with good intentions?"

"The best intentions in the world, I assure you."

"Are you armed?"

"No, señor; just this hunting knife. I always carry it, because of a vow."

"You can keep it then, that knife's not very sharp."

"Thanks."

"No need to thank me. Well, are we friends?"

"I certainly would like to be."

"Hold on a minute then, let's have something to drink."

The man took a wineskin down from the wall.

"Have some."

"You first."

"No, you first; I'm the host."

The traveler took a swallow of wine, which was harsh and oversweet, and passed the wineskin to the man.

"Listen here, I don't like to ask any more questions than I have to, but why didn't you stay in the town?"

The traveler doesn't know what to answer, and is evasive.

"Just a whim, I suppose you'd call it . . . I'm a little fed-up with towns and inns."

The man laughs.

"We have a very good one right here!"

"In Pareja?"

"Of course, man, did you think I meant Madrid? The inn on the plaza has the reputation of being very good."

The traveler gives him a look.

"Yes, so I've been told."

The man laughed again, took another drink, and heaved a sigh.

"Well, naturally I'd say it was! You know what they say about everything looking good to the eyes of love! One of the girls at the inn, María, it's a pity you didn't get to meet her, is going to marry me next spring, God willing. I'm getting pretty anxious, imagine sleeping here when I could be sleeping at the inn!"

In the light of the oil lamp the man's face looks like that of a blessed creature. With his imagination filled with golden ambitions, he seemed like an oversized, uncouth, wine-drinking cherub; a cherub lighted up from within by Grace.

The traveler had to fight down a slight feeling of envy.

"I hope you'll both be very happy."

"Thanks, I'm sure we will be."

9. CASASANA. CÓRCOLES. SACEDÓN.

TO GET to Sacedón from Pareja one goes along the same road the traveler took the day before, only in the opposite direction; and at the crossroads, just before the stream of Empolveda empties into the Tajo, one turns left in a southerly direction toward the Guadalajara-Cuenca highway. Sacedón is a little farther on in the direction of Cuenca.

One can also go the other way, that is away from the Tajo, through Escamilla and Millana, crossing the Altos del Llano and reaching the same highway at the level of Alcocer; this way passes through Córcoles and Sacedón, which is a good bit farther along in the direction of Guadalajara.

The way one emphatically does not go is by cutting across to Casasana. From Pareja to Casasana there is no highway, not even a local road, and one has to climb the steep slope by a goat track which at times is almost obliterated.

It goes without saying, naturally, that the traveler went by way of Casasana. He had to bring greetings to Fabián Gabarda, the brother of the woman he had met in Durón.

Casasana is a town set high up on a mountain called El Cerro de la Veleta, and built somewhat on the farther side, which is more level. You can't see Casasana until you're right on top of it. It is a very small town with little agriculture and a good deal of dairy stock: some eighty cows. Casasana was the only place in the Alcarria where the traveler found black-and-white milk cows of Dutch breed like the ones in Santander. They were, generally speaking, rather thin, but it was immediately obvious that they were of good stock.

The shortcut by which one climbs up to Casasana, called Roblegila, is devilish; it is as full of stones as a rockpile and very steep.

The sun is beating down strongly and the pack seems heavier than it ought to be. The slope is tiring, and halfway up, the traveler, who is sweating freely, decides that it would be well to make a stop and recover his energy. An old shepherd is sitting in the sun, wrapped up in a blanket which covers all but his head.

The traveler approaches him.

"Good day to you."

"God has given us a cool one today."

"Cool?"

"Stop walking and you'll see."

From this height, though Casasana is not yet visible, a broad and beautiful panorama can be seen. It is extremely varied, with great naked boulders and some small scanty herbage in the foreground, the red-and-white terrain of Pareja below and the green banks of the Tajo far off to the left.

And truly there is a sharp little wind up there that makes one shiver. The traveler feels a slight chill and starts walking again. Casasana soon appears, just as he comes to the top of the last slope. It has a very pretty color, ranging from a darkish green to a bluish gray. Two little girls are sitting in the sun tending a cow at the foot of the old Moorish castle, one wall of which serves as a handball court. As the traveler passes by, they get up and stare after him fixedly and ecstatically. They are poorly dressed and have great deep black eyes, full of charm and nobility. The traveler asks them what he knows already.

"Say, children, is this town Casasana?"

"Yes, señor, what else could it be?"

A woman goes by.

"Say, señora, where is the inn?"

"We have no inn in Casasana, señor."

The woman also has black eyes and black hair and a primitive beauty of a very ancient type, like all women of the town.

"In Durón I met a girl from Casasana who is married there;

she told me to ask for her mother. Her brother is a town councilman."

"Carmen Gabarda?"

"Yes."

"I'll take you, then. Her mother is the one who keeps the lodging house."

The traveler, who had already discovered that the usual word for an inn is unknown in the Alcarria, learns the difference between a lodging house and what he would call an inn. An inn is a lodging house with a stable to it. In Casasana, therefore, there is a lodging house but not an inn.

Carmen Gabarda's mother receives the traveler with a certain amount of reserve. In small towns the casual passerby is usually received well but somewhat coolly. They are twice shy, and they have reason. There have been cases of a man coming begging for something to eat in the name of charity—a sack of beans for his sick wife, for the love of God—and then he turned out to be an agent of the district tax office and there were affidavits and fines.

Fabián Gabarda is not at home; he is in the fields. The land around Casasana yields, among other things—wheat, barley, rye, oats, beans, chickpeas, almost everything and all in small quantities—tiny and very tasty olives which the people enjoy eating. Someone goes off to look for Fabián Gabarda and he soon arrives. He is a short, thin young man, sinewy and tough, who has hands like pliers. He is obliging and friendly and neither smokes nor drinks. In Casasana there are a great many young men who don't smoke or drink; the traveler thinks to himself that this must be something not very frequent in Spain.

The traveler washes up a little in the doorway of the house, while his meal is being prepared. Through the wall he hears the little girls in the school singing. The school in Casasana is shocking, a painfully poor school with the old benches covered with patches and mended places, the walls and ceiling with great blotches of dampness and a floor of badly cemented tiles which shift under the feet.

There are in the school, however—perhaps by way of compensation—great cleanliness, perfect order, and floods of sunlight.

A crucifix and a colored map of Spain are hanging from the wall, one of those maps that has the Canary Islands, the protectorate of Morocco, and the colonies of Río de Oro and the Gulf of Guinea in little squares at the bottom; to fit them all in doesn't require, really, more than a very small corner. There is a small Spanish flag in one corner of the room.

On the teacher's table are a few books, some notebooks and two vases of heavy greenish glass with some little yellow, red, and lilac-colored wild flowers in them. The teacher, who shows the traveler around the school, is a young and attractive girl with a certain look of the city about her; she has on lipstick and is wearing a very pretty flowered cotton dress. She speaks of teaching methods and tells the traveler that the children of Casasana are good pupils, that they work hard and are very intelligent. From outside the windows a group of boys and girls, silent, eyes wide with awe, are peeking into the school. The teacher calls to a boy and a girl.

"Come on now, so this gentleman can see you. Who discovered America?"

The boy doesn't hesitate for an instant.

"Christopher Columbus."

The teacher smiles.

"Now you; who was the best queen of Spain?"

"Isabella the Catholic."

"Why?"

"Because she fought against feudalism and Islam, brought about the unity of our country, and carried our religion and our culture beyond the seas."

The teacher, very pleased, explains to the traveler, "She's my best student."

The little girl is very solemn, very much impressed with her rôle of star pupil. The traveler gives her a caramel, takes her a little to one side and asks her, "What's your name?"

"Rosario González, to serve God and yourself."

"Fine. Now let's see, Rosario, do you know what feudalism is?"

"No, señor."

"And Islam?"

"No, señor. We don't have to learn that."

The little girl is somewhat alarmed and the traveler asks no more questions.

The traveler has an early lunch at about eleven and then goes to a tavern, one of the very few taverns in Casasana, to talk with some men who are taking a rest from their work. The people in Casasana are very hardworking, so much so that they are called "Squatters"; at least the rumor goes that they sleep in a squatting position so as to be able to get up early and go to the fields.

The traveler tries to find a man with some kind of pack animal to take his things to Sacedón, and after a great many consultations and comings and goings he reaches an agreement with a young man whom the others call Felipe the Tailor. Felipe is no tailor and neither were his father nor his grandfather, but the fact is, God only knows for what mysterious reason, the only name he is known by in the town is Felipe the Tailor.

Toward noon, with Felipe the Tailor and the donkey Lucero loaded with his gear, the traveler departs from Casasana to take the road of Los Chinarros, which will bring him as far as Córcoles. Fabián Gabarda and three or four other friends go with him as far as the meadow of Valdeloso, on the edge of town.

It is a splendid day, somewhat cloudy and not uncomfortably warm; the traveler, with no baggage to weigh him down, walks freely and joyfully.

The road of Los Chinarros describes a series of curves on its way down the mountain to Córcoles, and during the descent the traveler talks with Felipe of how fine the fields look and what a favorable year it promises to be.

"And about time too."

"I should say so."

Felipe is positively in love with the land and with agriculture; he holds ancient and wholesome opinions and has an intelligent knowledge of his business.

"Isn't it true that from up here this looks like Galicia?"

Near Córcoles they pass by the ivy-covered walls of a ruined convent surrounded by elms and walnut trees. A couple of dozen black sheep are grazing in the abandoned cloister. Some five or six black goats are clambering about the dilapidated walls, still miraculously in place, and a cloud of crows, black too of course, are cawing as they gobble away at the carcass of a donkey lying with its eyes open and its body swollen in the sun.

The traveler doesn't go into Córcoles; the town lies in front of him, a little to the left and somewhat away from the highway. The traveler goes to the right, toward Sacedón. As they come down to the plain the sun has begun to be troublesome and the traveler looks for some shade where he can sit down to rest for a while, to have something to drink, eat a bite, and smoke a cigarette.

There are anise fields of a brilliant green and well-tilled, still-young olive groves of an ashy green. Agriculture in Córcoles is rich and prosperous and its inhabitants have lived well since they bought their lands, undoubtedly for much less than they were worth, from the Count of Arcentales; nowadays everyone in Córcoles is a landowner and everyone lives off his own property. The people speak with affection and respect of the Count of Arcentales and are pleased with the purchase.

"Then selling it was a bad piece of business for the gentleman."

"No, señor, neither good nor bad. The count never intended it to be a matter of business, he wanted to favor the townspeople. The only loss we've had out of it is that now he almost never comes here. Before, he used to come every year and used to have bread baked and meat killed for everyone."

Felipe laments the fact that the land in Casasana is poor.

"This is entirely different, it's pleasanter and easier to work. Up there we work our guts out on the land and still stay poor. Of course, if we didn't work hard we'd be worse off, don't you agree?"

"Yes."

Felipe is sad and thoughtful.

"These people here had all the luck!"

"Yes, more than a little, certainly."

Felipe raises his eyes.

"You know what I say? All the better for them then and may

God preserve it for them; I'm not like some folks, I'm not envious."

Between the highway and the town are some well-kept garden plots. A few men are bent over the ground working and others are resting in the shade of a tree beside their unyoked mules.

"If this land were mine, I'd never rest; I'd hardly even sleep."

Felipe is an energetic man who would have made a good emigrant and perhaps a good colonizer.

"Do you come from rich land or poor?"

"Rich land, I'd say."

"Up toward Valladolid or Salamanca?"

"No, farther north; up in Galicia."

Felipe snaps his fingers.

"That's pure Heaven!"

"Do you know that part of the world?"

"No, but I've heard a lot about it; I was with Galicians all during the war. D'you know one named Pepito Ferreiro?"

"No, can't say I do."

"Well, we were great friends; he and I always went around together and the day I got shot he did too; it was in the Alcubierre mountains in the province of Zaragoza."

"I'll be damned! Say, what do you think of us Galicians?"

"Fine people, very hardworking and very loyal. But just the same, you know, you people have a bad reputation here in Castile."

"So what can we do about it?"

"I don't say it to flatter you, but what I think is that it's just ignorance."

"Maybe so!"

As the traveler approaches Sacedón, vineyards and oxen pulling ploughs begin to appear. Mule carts go up and down and an occasional truck passes, loaded to the utmost. Sometimes the Civil Guard stops one of the trucks; they're apt to carry black-market stuff under the load.

More and more people come into view and, still a league and a half away from Sacedón, the traveler begins to meet folk returning from the fields, walking in the ditch in groups of three or four with hoes on their shoulders and a dog running behind, some with a golden gourd slung from a shoulder strap or hanging from their waists. It is quite late in the afternoon, and eventually the highway looks like a city street, except that all the traffic is going in the same direction.

At the edge of town there is a beautiful avenue of male and female elms. The male trees are the ones with pointed tops and the female ones have round thick maternal branches.

Once in Sacedón, the traveler takes the shortcut which goes past the cemetery, a path which will soon disappear beneath the waters of a canal already under construction. To the left, on the way up, is a factory for pressing olive wastes, La Orujera, with its tall chimney puffing smoke like a locomotive. Sacedón, which is surrounded by fields of fresh green wheat, appears to be a town of some importance and an industrious one. It is fairly spread out and the tower of the church stands out gracefully above the houses.

In the ball court the young fellows are busy playing handball. There are a good many onlookers but nobody, except for two or three very young boys, shouts any encouragement to the players. The spectators limit themselves to watching silently but attentively, and smoking cigarettes. As always happens, there is a left-handed player—whom, naturally, they call Lefty—who is the best of all; the traveler, who doesn't know much about the game, thinks that it must be very confusing to have your opponent play wrong-handed.

By the time the traveler reaches the plaza it is almost dark. Some traveling traders with long whips and caps with lavender and pink visors are presiding over a litter of about two dozen piglets as black as coal and as wiggly as babies. The piglets must be some two months old and have recently been weaned; there are probably three or four of them to a twenty-five pound measure, and the owners are asking from seven hundred to eight hundred and fifty pesetas apiece, depending on whether they are male or female. Odd though it seems, the females are worth less than the males. It's customary to buy them for the butchering, because the male pig is the most marvelous of creatures;

in seven months, with a little luck, he'll weigh two hundred and seventy-five or three hundred pounds and be worth four thousand pesetas.

The traveler sits down on a stone bench in the plaza, with his back to the inn where he is going to sleep, to rest in the cool of the evening and talk with Felipe the Tailor.

"Now, here's a town that's really rich!"

"Yes, it does seem to be."

"It sure is! In Sacedón it's not like in some other towns; here everybody, great and small, goes to bed with a full belly."

Before long the bus arrives; none of the towns which the traveler visited had the railroad except Guadalajara. The bus opens its doors and the passengers come pouring out in great haste; it is obvious that they have been uncomfortable. A crowd of girls and children swarm around the travelers, making a deafening racket. The patrons of the bus are extremely varied in appearance: an interminable family of gypsies, some pale skinny children who have come to spend a few days with their country cousins, a few rich, well-dressed peasant girls, a trader or two in a long black smock with a silk handkerchief at the throat.

The traveler thinks that, just in case, the most prudent thing to do is to go over to the inn and order his supper and arrange for a bed. The inn is an overgrown house of unusual depth. Over the arch of the doorway is written "Parador"; on one corner, on a little porcelain plaque, "Street of Doctor Ramón y Cajal"; and above the balconies and spreading over the whole façade, "Parador de Francisco Pérez." Francisco Pérez is dead now and the inn is kept by his son Antonio Pérez. The traveler regrets that the present owner hasn't put his name on the façade; he would have felt quite excited about sleeping in an inn called "Parador de Antonio Pérez,"* such a short distance from Pastrana.

In the entrance way the traveler bumps into Martín, the salesman he met in Trillo and saw again in Budia.

*Antonio Pérez (*ca.* 1540–1611). Minister of Philip II and lover of Ana de Mendoza, Princess of Eboli (1540–1592). Involved in court intrigue, he escaped to Aragon and later to France; the princess was imprisoned and died in Pastrana. [Translator's note.]

"I thought you wouldn't be coming."

"Well, here I am."

"I've been here since yesterday."

"Yes, but you came on your bicycle. Do you think they'll have a bed for me?"

"Sure, come and see the landlord's wife. I've already told her you'd come."

The landlord's wife is a plump young woman, the picture of health, and rosy as an apple.

"I've already been told you'd be coming."

The traveler smiled at the salesman. The woman continued, "You won't find anything fancy here, just good will and everything nice and clean."

"Fine."

"Now what do you want for supper? I don't have much but you're welcome to it: eggs, some nice young veal, trout, some things left over from the butchering, a few potatoes on the side . . . For dessert you can have canned pineapple or brandied cherries; if you want fresh fruit I can give you some, and if you like cheese I'd be surprised if I couldn't find a little for you somewhere. I don't have much in the way of wine, but there ought to be some bottled Rioja left."

The traveler is startled, absolutely speechless. The woman speaks as though she were apologizing; she must think she has a duke in her house. There's no doubt that the salesman had given him splendid advance billing. The only trouble with being taken for a rich man comes when it's time to pay up.

While the supper is being prepared the traveler and his friend go to the café to have some vermouth. The café is jampacked and the air could be cut with a knife. People are playing dominoes at some tables and cards at others. Over in a corner two solitary types are having a game of chess; they look grave, solemn, and disdainful. Three or four onlookers who seem to be functioning as toadies are sitting silently beside them; when one of the players takes out a cigarette the nearest looker-on lights it for him; when he makes a vague motion toward the waiter, the first looker-on to notice takes it on himself to signal with a loud and angry "pssst!"; when a pawn or bishop or knight rolls under the table, the looker-on whose turn it is hastens to retrieve it. It must be very comfortable for the players.

The traveler is ill at ease in the café.

"As soon as we finish our vermouth let's go, shall we?"

"As you like."

On the street, by the light from a store window, some little girls are standing in a circle singing:

> "I am the widow of Count Laurel
> Who I'll marry nobody can tell."

Felipe the Tailor is in the doorway of the inn talking to some mule drivers. The donkey has been given an armload of feed and put in the stable. When the traveler comes in, Felipe goes up to him.

"I guess I can go now."

"Not now, man! You can rest awhile and go back early tomorrow. I'm inviting you to supper."

"Don't bother, I brought something with me."

"What of it? Keep it for the road. You're going to have supper with this friend and me."

"Well, all right, since you insist!"

Felipe the Tailor, Martín the salesman, and the traveler had their supper in a small, extremely clean, well-furnished dining room; a dining room which it was easy to see was opened only on special occasions. During the supper a red-haired man of about fifty, with sideburns and thick glasses, burst into the dining room, glared at the traveler, and asked him pointblank, "Listen, you, do you sell soda-bottle caps?"

"No, I certainly don't."

"You never have sold them?"

"No, señor. I have never sold soda-bottle caps."

The man made a gesture of resignation, turned on his heel and departed. The landlord's wife explained to the traveler later that two or three years before, the eyeglassed, sideburned man, who had a little soft-drink factory in Priego de Cuenca, had been sent a shipment of five thousand caps, all of them rusted.

"The salesman who sent them was a good deal like you, tall and brown-haired."

After a stupendous supper, the traveler lights a cigar which doesn't draw. He tries putting a jacket on it but it still refuses to draw. In view of this fact he leaves it almost intact in a metal ashtray full of butts, with a scene from *Don Quixote* on it in relief. The three men sit around the table talking for a while and the traveler helps his friend the salesman work out his next itinerary with a Michelin guide. The salesman is delighted.

"With my iron donkey I'd go all the way to Siberia. I've already made up my mind: get rich or bust!"

Felipe the Tailor took his departure to sleep for a bit and the two friends went out to take a turn around the town.

"Shall we have some coffee?"

"Sure, whatever you say."

They took their coffee standing up at the counter in the café.

"Now, if you feel like it, we can go and say hello to a friend of mine. He's a good fellow and I haven't seen him for quite a while."

"All right, let's go."

Martín's friend had a bicycle-renting business. Martín made the introduction: "This is a gentleman from Madrid; this is Paco, we all call him 'Blue Streak.' If this kid really trained he'd be another champion like Delio Rodríguez."

Paco, "Blue Streak," was in his shop with his friends clustered around him. He was something of a popular hero and undoubtedly one of the best cyclists in the province. The group was talking about the Tour of Spain.

"Carretero's not the man he used to be, anybody can see that, and Delio . . . look, sheer grit is what puts him among the winners. He has a good team, that's all; the man who races alone doesn't have a chance, he might as well stay home."

The traveler nods agreement to everything.

Sacedón is a town where people stay up till all hours, at least at this time of year. Twelve o'clock has already struck when the friends return to the inn, and there are still groups of people silently taking the air on the benches of the plaza and in the doorways of the houses.

In the entrance way of the inn ten or twelve mule drivers and traders are sleeping, wrapped in their blankets; the owner of the soft-drink factory is snoring in a corner and Felipe the Tailor is reposing nearby, curled up in a ball.

A good deal of bustling about can still be heard in the kitchen. The owner's wife and two maids are moving here and there, drying plates and putting things in their places. Beside the dying fire a man is dozing and a cat sleeping. The copper ladles glisten from the walls, polished to the last degree, and the aluminum pans are ranged on the shelf in order of size.

The traveler says good night to the landlady and goes up to his room. Martín is evasive, and departs; the traveler had overheard a chance remark in the bicycle shop which seemed to indicate that Martín was a man who had considerable luck with women. The traveler made a half-joking reference to this and Martín preened like a pigeon; he could hardly contain himself for pride.

The traveler had an outside room with a large balcony overlooking the plaza—or rather, the Street of Doctor Ramón y Cajal—with two beds and a washbowl in it. On the floor beside the bed the traveler found his baggage, carefully arranged. On the night table was a pretty vase full of blue flowers with brown stems and green leaves, and from under the bed loomed a monumental porcelain chamber pot of well over a quart in capacity. The traveler looked under the other bed and saw a miserable little pot, all chipped, lusterless, worn-out and puny.

Once in bed, the traveler smoked a cigarette and turned out the light. He was tired and lost no time in going to sleep. The bed was clean and the mattress splendid, and the traveler slept deliciously, without alarms or nightmares, for nine hours in a row.

The other bed was unused. Martín had apparently hit the mark.

When he went down to breakfast the traveler found Martín, carefully shaved and combed, with a clean shirt and shiny shoes, sitting in the dining room reading the newspaper.

"I always read this paper, it has a lot of local news in it."

The paper was *El Alcázar* of Madrid, Guadalajara edition.

Martín, assiduous as always, went to the kitchen door to tell them to bring breakfast. The metal ashtray, now freshly cleaned, was on the table, and in the middle of the ashtray, proud and solitary as any queen, was the cigar butt the traveler had left the night before; it was really a most impressive butt.

During breakfast—fried eggs with bacon, café-au-lait with bread and butter, and fruit—the traveler talks to Martín.

"How did things go last night?"

Martín smiles, looking like a mischievous schoolboy, and makes no reply. Before he leaves, the traveler goes out to the kitchen to see the landlord's wife.

"Listen, señora, I'm going to take a walk around town and then I'll be leaving Sacedón. Would you mind giving me a bill?"

"Certainly, señor, I have it all written down, it's fifty-five pesetas."

"No, charge it all to me, the supper for my two friends last night and Señor Martín's breakfast this morning, because I told him he was my guest."

"Yes, señor, it's all put down: thirty-six pesetas for the supper, five for the bed, and twelve pesetas for the two breakfasts; I put on two pesetas for service to round it off."

The traveler looked at the bill, for the sake of formality, and paid. He tried to give a five-peseta tip but she refused to take it.

"May I leave my knapsack here till I come back for it?"

"Of course, señor, I'll keep it in the kitchen."

The traveler went out to take a little turn around the town. Sacedón is a handsome town with wide, open streets. There are a good many three-story houses and many well-supplied business establishments. Martín explains to him which are clients of his and which are not.

A tanner has a marten's pelt stuffed with straw at the door of his shop as an advertisement. The tanner is a foxy old fellow, crafty and sly. He is affable and smiling but he never misses a trick.

"Nowadays it's not like it used to be; these days you really have to sweat to make any kind of a living."

His name is Pío and the unkind nickname he goes by is Uncle Cat. He is small, stubble-chinned, and squinty; he has on a rough leather apron and wears a filthy beret with no tab on top. His shop is small too and it is foul smelling, shabby, and jumbled. The scraping tool is hanging on the wall; the copper knife is resting on a table awaiting its time to devour the grain of the leather; the skinning knife, the scalpel, and the scraper prick up their ears from above some stuffed bull's testicles; the casks of wood chips and of tannin rest in a corner.

"Have much work?"

"Not a thing, don't pay any attention to all that gear; a man can hardly make enough to get along."

Later Martín explains to the traveler that Uncle Cat has a reputation in the town of being a rich man, even a millionaire.

An idiot is sitting in the sun stuffing himself with apricots.

"Look at that fellow; there's one who really understands life."

"Well, he does and he doesn't!"

When he reaches the plaza the traveler sees a bus just getting ready to depart, and he has a base thought. He goes and gets his pack and says goodbye to the landlord's wife.

"I hope you're going away pleased?"

"Yes, señora, very pleased."

"Have we given you good service?"

"Very good, yes indeed."

"All right then, you know where to find us."

"Don't worry, I won't forget."

"Are you going on the bus?"

The traveler turns a shamefaced pink.

"Yes, but only a little way."

"As far as the Tendilla crossroads?"

"That's right, as far as the Tendilla crossroads."

10. A TRIP BY BUS

Traveling by bus, the flight is gallinaceous.

José Pla

THE bus is loaded to the limit and room is made for the traveler in the last row of seats, among some gypsies. The traveler had found gypsies everywhere in the Alcarria, gypsies who live in peace and perfect harmony with the countryfolk, gypsies who are hard workers and good craftsmen—*churumajós* who can put a good sole on a shoe, *patalarós* who sing flamenco airs in the forges, *cascaroberós* who produce the shiniest pots, *bajirinanós* who make light, durable baskets—gypsies with a fixed residence who are on the lists of the Civil Register, do their military service, and travel by bus; the only thing they do not do is marry outside their race.

The traveler, as he tries to get settled in the seat, unintentionally steps on the foot of a very handsome young gypsy girl. She screeches, "May a drunken Englishman punch you in the nose, you clod!"

When the bus starts off, the people try to adjust to each other. The adjustment is sometimes painful.

"Hey, you're squashing my baby!"

The man addressed, trying to keep his balance, answers without looking back; he couldn't turn his head if he tried.

"Toss it up on the baggage rack, señora, and keep your mouth shut."

"We'd have to wait till August for that, right now I've still got him inside of me."

No sooner has the bus got out of town than some servant girls begin to make a racket; it turns out that they keep it up for the whole trip. Before the bus reaches the Tajo a fat lady says "Excuse me," and vomits all over a civil guardsman, his wife, and a nursing baby she is carrying. The baby had been asleep but, as is only natural, it wakes up and begins to cry; the baby squalls as though it were being murdered. After all, as a young man in a bow tie and a light-green soft hat remarks so sensibly, the incident was hardly worth making such a fuss about.

The maids sing without stopping for a moment, though they do change songs constantly. They began with "Amapola, My Pretty Amapola" and then went on with "Where Are Our Wandering Boys Tonight?", with "Rose of Madrid, the Flower of Chamberí," the "Addis Ababa March" in a special arrangement, and "The Bald-Headed Girl Without Any Hair."

Beside the driver are a non-commissioned officer of the Civil Guard, a cavalry sergeant, and a solemn gentlemen in black who looks as if he might be a lawyer's clerk.

People are talking about the reservoirs which are being made on the Tajo and the Guadiela. To judge from what is said, they are going to be very important ones. From the outskirts of Sacedón, the mountain range of San Cristóbal can be seen, dark green in color and not very high. A goatherd is tending his flock on some land which will soon be swallowed up by the waters. At the foot of the mountains some cement factories have been built for the purpose of supplying the work on the reservoir.

If the traveler had gone on foot he could have come through the shortcut of Entrepeña, which will also disappear under the water.

The young man in the bow tie and soft hat explains to the traveler, as he twists his body unmercifully to be able to look straight at him, that—just imagine!—the reservoir of Entrepeña and that of Guadiela are going to be connected by an underwater tunnel so they will level each other "mutually." The traveler agrees, but without much conviction; to tell the truth, whether or not the reservoirs of Entrepeña and Guadiela level each other is a matter of very little concern to him.

Just on the other side of the Tajo some newly constructed buildings come into view, the storage sheds and the homes of the engineers; they have a dreary, public-works appearance, a vulgar assembly-line look about them. The highway is one continuous curve and the nauseated lady now has two imitators who are hanging halfway out the windows. The poor ladies had to climb right over the passengers to get to the windows.

As the bus passes through Auñón, the maids have got as far as "Rose of Madrid." One of them, fat and sexy and bold-looking, yells "Hooray for my boyfriend!" The others, who seem more decent girls, content themselves with "Hooray for my village!" or "Hooray for me!", which is one hooray that is never out of place.

Generally speaking, the landscape is green and wooded and continues to be so until after they pass Alhóndiga, near the road-menders' hut at the crossroads which turns off to Fuentelaencina; then the bare plateau begins again.

Alhóndiga is a town built mostly of adobe brick and almost suspended above the river Arlés, which descends from the peak of Berninches in the mountain range behind El Olivar.

The traveler asks the driver what he has to do to get to Pastrana.

"Well, you can go along as far as the Tendilla crossroads and wait for the other bus there, the one that comes from Madrid."

"What time does it pass?"

"Around seven or seven-thirty in the evening."

As it is only eleven in the morning and, to judge from the map, it's not much more than a league farther on from Tendilla to the crossroads, the traveler decides to get off in Tendilla to see a little of the town and have lunch, and then get to the crossroads on foot.

Two or three kilometers before reaching Tendilla, at the left of the highway, are some run-of-the-mill ruins; the traveler doesn't know whether or not they are historic but he does know that they didn't look very interesting.

The approach to the town, on the banks of a stream which bears the same name, is along a very attractive and fairly luxuriant poplar grove.

The gypsies are asleep and as he gets off the bus the traveler has to wake them up in order to get out.

"Goodbye, señores, have a good trip."

"Goodbye to you too, and good luck."

As he reaches the ground the traveler realizes that both legs have gone to sleep and that he can hardly walk. His back hurts and his clothes are all twisted and pulled out of place. The bus has stopped in front of a tavern and the traveler goes in to have a drink and to put his clothing back where it belongs, bit by bit.

Tendilla is a town which has a plaza lined with flat columns; it is long, like a sausage, and stretched out all along the highway. This is the town where the writer Don Pío Baroja has an olive grove, so that he can have oil all the year.

The traveler talks with the girls in the tavern.

"Do you know Pío Baroja?"

"No, señor."

"And you don't know who he is?"

"No, señor, we don't."

The mother, who has come out of the kitchen, breaks in, "Yes, dears, of course; he's the gentleman Eufrasia works for, the one who bought that land on the Moratilla path; it's next to Uncle Squandercart's field."

"Oh, sure! But that gentleman never comes here, he must be very old; the secretary says he's a very important gentleman, important as can be."

After chatting for a time the traveler goes out to find a place to leave his baggage and to have a look at the town. He passes in front of an inn which has a lettered board hanging from a balcony: the board reads: "Parador Antiguo de Juan Nuevo," which means "Old Inn of Juan New." The traveler goes in, but nobody comes to greet him except a skinny, decrepit bitch who barks at him impolitely and shows her teeth in a snarl. The traveler expects either that someone will emerge or that the dog will shut up, but she doesn't stop barking and no owner makes an appearance. The traveler steps inside the doorway and claps his hands a couple of times. The bitch becomes even more infuriated and makes a determined effort to bite his legs. The traveler stepped back and gave her such a kick, it's a wonder he didn't smash her against the wall. Poor thing, what a tremendous kick she took! The dog began to howl and limped off vanquished. A woman came out, roused by the howls.

"What have you done to Perlita?"

"Never mind, señora, and skip the questions! Can I eat here?"

"I've got nothing to eat, get out of here! If you don't go in a hurry I'll call my Juan and he'll drive you out at the end of a stick!"

"Stop yelling, señora, don't waste your breath. You needn't call your Juan, I'm going."

Back on the street again, the traveler found a child to serve as guide and went clear to the other end of the town, where he found a very spruce little establishment with tiled floors and gilt-framed photographs on the walls. The landlady was a friendly sort of woman who promised to fix the traveler a partridge for his lunch. The traveler went out to the barnyard, took a pail of water out of the well and began to wash up. There were a great many fowl in the yard, and of all varieties: doves, a couple of dozen hens, about the same number of ducks, six or seven turkeys, and two beautiful geese. When the traveler was bending over to splash some water on the back of his neck, one of the geese gave him such a tremendous peck on the buttocks that if it didn't take off a chunk of flesh it was because it misjudged the distance and hit bone. The traveler got the scare of his life—for nobody expects to get such a whopping bite on the behind while he's washing—and uttered a somewhat immoderate yell. The barnyard went into a frenzy: the doves took off; the hens and ducks began to scurry frantically from one place to another; the geese honked like demons; the landlady appeared on the scene to see what had happened, and the traveler, one hand clutching a stick and the other the place where it hurt, was in the process of trying to decide whether to flee or to attack the foe.

"What's happened?"

"As you can see, señora, if I'm not careful I won't be able to sit down for the rest of my life."

"A goose, wasn't it?"

"Yes, señora, it was a goose all right."

"It's because they don't know you, of course! Is it bleeding?"

The traveler felt himself tenderly.

"No, señora, it appears not."

The turkeys were the only ones who kept calm. The traveler left the barnyard and reflected that the animals in that particular town were somewhat unnecessarily fierce. Maybe the popular saying that begins, "Buy no mule in Tendilla" was invented to preserve mule drivers from being kicked to death. Who knows? At any rate, the anonymous author of the proverb takes the precaution of warning, a little further on, that the mule will turn out to be unreliable.

The traveler went and took a walk till one o'clock, when his lunch would be ready. On the road to the cemetery he saw some very pretty walls with ivy growing in some of the corners, the remains of an ancient convent. Near it on a piece of level ground overlooking the valley there was a stone cross, not tall but very graceful. The whole farming area of Tendilla is visible from there, with its olive groves on the hillsides and its garden plots on the plain, bordering the highway and the stream.

After lunch the traveler started walking slowly toward the crossroads. He didn't meet a living soul in the league he walked, nor did he see anything which particularly impressed him. The landscape along there is darkish, monotonous, and boring, and it seems as though people deliberately keep from going there.

At the Tendilla crossroads there is a lunch bar with a grape arbor and a porch all covered with a blooming, fresh, and sweet-smelling climbing vine. They have bottles of cold beer—which they cool by putting them in a pail down the well and keeping them there for hours and hours—and they serve good sausage and bread for snacks. That little place in the middle of the countryside was really a good deal like the Garden of Eden.

They brought a folding canvas chair out to the arbor for the traveler, and there he ate his bread and sausage, drank his beer, took a little nap and waited for the bus which was to take him to Pastrana.

The woman who kept the place was pleasant and knew her job, and the traveler, sprawled in a chaise longue and enjoying the supreme luxury of a restful day, felt absolutely happy; he noticed that his imagination was flooded with a swarm of golden thoughts, and at last he slept the sleep of the blest, perhaps even with a smile on his lips.

The bus awakened him from his sweet slumbers, arriving more than half an hour before its usual time. The people who were going to wait for the bus to Sacedón got off and almost half the seats were left vacant.

The bus started off along the road to Fuentelviejo because its usual route, a highway branching off to the right, was in bad shape and even impassable in places because of flooding. Fuentelviejo is a small pretty town, very characteristic of the region. A young newly married couple who had spent their honeymoon in Guadalajara got off there.

Along the roadside are caves, each with a seat dug out of the earth and a sort of little porch made of dry branches. The landscape is rolling and green. When the bus reaches the side road that goes to Moratilla de los Meleros, it stops to let off three or four people who will then climb the scant kilometer which separates them from the village.

"It was lucky for you we went this way!" the driver says to them.

"Man, that's one good thing the floods have done!"

As far as Hueva the highway runs between very carefully cultivated little garden plots. Hueva has a church with a leaning tower, like Pisa. The bus is almost empty now and the passengers are beginning to collect their bundles, their suitcases, their bags and baskets.

"Are you from Pastrana?"

"No, señor."

"Traveling salesman, maybe?"

"No, señor, I'm not."

"Ah! Then maybe you're going to visit one of the prisoners?"

11. PASTRANA

THE traveler arrives in Pastrana just as darkness is falling. The bus discharges him on the outskirts of town at the top of a long steep hill which it refuses to descend, perhaps so that it won't have to make the climb again next day loaded with men and women, military men and civilians, trunks, baskets, cartons, bags, and hatboxes.

It is a poor time to have reached the town and the traveler decides to look for a place to stay, have supper, go to bed, and leave the rest for next day. The morning light is preferable and more propitious for this matter of wandering through a town, talking with people, taking a good look at things, and writing down an occasional note or impression in a notebook. It even seems that in the mornings people look more favorably on a stranger, that they are less suspicious, trust him more readily, and are more inclined to give him some piece of information he asks for, a glass of water he requests or a cigarette paper he needs. At night people are tired and the darkness makes them fearful, mistrustful, and guarded. In the morning, on the other hand, especially when summer is just beginning and the days are longer, the light clearer, and the weather milder, people seem to be kinder and more appproachable, and towns have a more cheerful and optimistic and jovial air.

The nighttime seems to have been made for stealing, silently and with stealthy tread, the bag of gold coins which every family keeps at the bottom of a chest among the linen sheets, the aromatic dried quinces, and the Manila shawls; the morning, by contrast, seems especially provided for begging alms heartily and shamelessly, with a smile on the lips and hands in the pockets.

"Can you give me five centimos?"

"God keep you, brother; I can't."

"That's all right, somebody else'll give it to me."

To first go into a town or a house at night is bad; the traveler has some experience on this subject and knows that he has always had better luck in the towns he got to by daylight.

As he thinks about this he is walking down toward the plaza, without looking around him very much. He is searching for an inn and surely in the plaza he can get some information. He doesn't require much and needs no luxuries. Pastrana is a large town and probably has half-a-dozen places, either inns or hotels or lodgings, to choose from.

The plaza is full of groups of men who are chatting, and girls who are walking about surrounded by young civil guardsmen who court and woo them. Pastrana has a large detachment of the Civil Guard. Some little boys are playing ball in one corner and some little girls are skipping rope in another. There is an occasional young blade in a necktie and an occasional girl in high heels. The streetlights are just beginning to go on and the noisy crackle of a radio issues from a nearby balcony.

The traveler approaches a group of men.

"Good evening."

"Good evening to you."

The man who speaks turns out to be the mayor. After he and the traveler have talked for a while they discover that they are friends. No one has introduced them, but that's beside the point. They don't even know each other's names, though that matter is easy enough to clear up.

The traveler gives his name and the mayor gives his in turn; the mayor's name is Don Mónico Fernández Toledano, and he is a lawyer and the business manager of the Count. The Count, naturally, is the Count of Romanones.

Don Mónico is an intelligent and cordial man, somewhat heavy-set, fairly short, an omnivorous reader, an easy conversationalist, and not overfond of writing letters, as he himself confesses. Don Mónico is an old-fashioned mayor who runs his town like a paterfamilias and has a classic and practical sense of hospitality and authority. It occurs to the traveler that the mayors of past times, who were appointed by the king, must have been a good deal like Don Mónico; he has no idea whether they were good or bad but he imagines them all to have been upright, romantic, and patriarchal.

Don Mónico wants to show the traveler something of the town, but the traveler has a vague superstitious feeling and refuses.

"Let's go see it tomorrow, I'm a little tired at the moment."

"Whatever you say. Let's have a vermouth then."

In the town club, which is on the plaza, the mayor and the traveler sit down at an empty table. The traveler puts his pack on the floor and the mayor calls the headwaiter and orders two vermouths and some olives, asks him to take the traveler's things to the inn and tell them to prepare a bed for one and supper for three, and instructs him to locate Don Paco.

The card players nod greetings to the mayor and glance casually at the traveler.

The vermouth and olives are not slow in appearing and Don Paco arrives without delay. Don Paco is a young, well-dressed man with a high color and a cultured air about him, rather thoughtful looking, and with a smile which is faintly, imperceptibly, remotely sad.

"Were you asking for me?"

"Yes. I wanted to introduce you; this is a friend who's taking a walking trip through these parts; and this is Don Francisco Cortijo Ayuso, my second-in-command."

Don Paco is a doctor; his conversation is sensible, his gaze reflective, and his views are quiet and to the point.

"And how does our town look to you?"

"I haven't seen it yet. I'd rather see it tomorrow morning, in daylight."

"Yes, I think that would be better too."

Don Mónico, Don Paco, and the traveler talked at length of many things, of everything that came into their heads, and the three of them consumed a great many vermouths and a great many stuffed olives. By the time they rose from the table there was nobody left in the club, and by the time they sat down to supper in the hotel, they really weren't very hungry any more . . .

Next morning, when the traveler made his appearance in the Plaza de la Hora and felt that he had entered Pastrana in spirit and in truth, the first sensation he had was one of being in a medieval city, a great medieval city. The Plaza de la Hora is square, large, uncluttered, and airy. It is a curious plaza, for it has only three sides, the fourth being open and commanding a view down to one of the two river meadows of the Arlés. On the Plaza de la Hora is the palace of the dukes, where the Princess of Eboli was kept prisoner and where she died. The palace is distressing to look at. The façade is still more or less intact but the interior is completely in ruins. In the room where the Princess died—a sort of cell with a finely wrought iron grille, on the upper floor of the right wing of the building—the National Wheat Service has set up shop; there are heaps of grain on the floor and a scale for weighing the sacks. The room has a frieze of very beautiful tiles, historic tiles which saw the Princess die, but many have fallen off and with every day that passes there will be fewer of them; the mule drivers and peasants, during the tedious wait to present their sworn declarations, while away the time by digging them out with their knives. The immense room beside it, which occupies almost all the central part of the façade, still retains some remnants of a noble carved wooden ceiling which threatens to fall down from one day to another.

A mule cart is being loaded in the courtyard; a few hens are pecking away at the ground and others are scratching in a heap of manure; two boys are playing with sticks and a dog is lying in the sun looking bored.

The traveler does not know who the present owners of the palace may be—some tell him it belongs to the family of the dukes, others that it is the property of the State or of the Jesuits—but he is of the opinion that it must belong to someone who has little love for Pastrana, for the palace, or for the Princess of Eboli, individually or collectively.

It was in this palace that a former priest of the town, Don Eustoquio García Merchante, once attempted to establish a museum. There was sufficient material to begin one and the plan was to try to find more. The most important item would have been, of course, the famous collection of tapestries of Alfonso V of Portugal.

Don Eustoquio's idea did not have the acceptance which it merited, the project withered on the vine, and Pastrana remained museumless; it will soon have no palace; and the tapestries took flight and are now in Madrid. Don Eustoquio has left witness of his attempt in a book entitled *The Tapestries of Alfonso V of Portugal, Now Housed in the Former Collegiate Church of Pastrana,* printed by the Editorial Católica Toledana, Street of San Juan Labrador, No. 6, in 1929.

Today, as has been said, the tapestries are no longer in the former Collegiate Church of Pastrana. The citizens of Pastrana have requested their return numerous times, but their pleas fall on empty air. Their argument is uncontestable—give us back our own—but the answer always is that Pastrana has no suitable place for them and that they were deteriorating in the sacristy where they were kept.

The traveler considers that this is a quarrel which is none of his business, but he also thinks that this mania for putting all the worthwhile things into museums in Madrid is ruining the provinces which are, after all, the nation. Things are always best seen when they are a trifle mixed-up, a trifle disordered; the chilly administrative neatness of museums and filing cases, of statistics and cemeteries, is an unhuman and antinatural kind of order; it is, in a word, disorder. True order belongs to Nature, which never yet has produced two identical trees or mountains or horses. Furthermore, to have taken the tapestries out of Pastrana and brought them to the capital was a mistake; it's much more pleasant to come upon things as it were by chance than to go look at them in a place where you know they'll be set up to perfection, with no risk of disappointment. However, . . .

There are two exits to the Puerta de la Hora. The one on the left, as you stand with your back to the palace, leads to the former Moorish quarter of El Albaicín; the one on the right, to the Christian quarter of San Francisco.

The traveler sets forth to explore the city and walks through streets of ancient names, streets paved with tiny cobblestones and lined with houses which have nail-studded doors with heavy iron hardware and balconies adorned with pots of geraniums, carnations, asparagus plant, and sweet basil. Pastrana is a city of streets with beautiful, evocative names: Street of the Ladies, of the Bull, of the Chimneys, Street of Santa María, of the Height, of the Pool, of the Fig Orchard, of the Threshing Floor, of Moratín.

Moratín wrote his comedy *El sí de las niñas* in Pastrana, and married there for the second time; it's a pity too that something wasn't done to preserve the house he lived in.

In the plaza of Cuatro Caños the traveler discovers a slender fountain shaped like a goblet, covered with a stone veneer now cracked by the passage of time, and surmounted by a decoration in the form of a chess pawn. Water no longer flows from the fountain and some unattractive weeds are growing in the cracks of the stone. The mayor arranges to have water come out of the spouts so that the traveler can take a picture, and sends a constable off to find a wrench to open them with. Several women take advantage of the circumstance to fill their pitchers and jugs.

The portico of the church of Our Lady of the Assumption bears a garland of tea roses. The church is closed and the priest is not at home; he has gone out for a little walk. After a great deal of searching and asking of questions, the sexton is located. The sexton and the traveler explore the church together; it must have been an important one at one time. The sexton is one of the learned kind and explains to the traveler a great many things which he promptly forgets again. In the church lies buried the hermit Juan de Buenavida y Buencuchillo, who must have been quite a character and who, according to report, is going to be beatified; the traveler thinks that his astonishing name, Good Life and Good Knife, is worthy of one of those ballads sung by blind beggars; it is a name more appropriate to a bandit or a feudal lord than to a future Blessed.

The church is very historic and is laden with the memory of noble deeds long past, but the traveler considers that undoubtedly the most beautiful thing about it is the portico with its tea rose bush. At one time the church had a choir of some forty canons and prebendaries, but nowadays, perhaps because they didn't know how to hold on to a good thing when they had it, the choir stalls are empty and not a man remains.

Pastrana recalls Toledo in an indefinable way, and occasionally Santiago de Compostela too. It has clear and evident points of contact with Toledo; a little street, a doorway, a street corner, the color of a façade, even an occasional cloud formation. With Santiago it has only a kind of vague similarity of feeling; the traveler doesn't know how to explain it in any other way.

Pastrana, which once was a city with a strong ecclesiastical tradition, is today almost devoid of clergy. The chapter of its Collegiate Church was said to be equaled only by that of the Cathedral of Toledo, and its convent of Discalced Carmelites was founded by St. Theresa and once lodged St. John of the Cross.

Today the chapter has disappeared and the convent is of no importance.

The convent can be seen from the Plaza de la Hora; it stands on a height, above the place where the two meadows of the Arlés meet. The traveler and his two friends walk first along the highway and then go along a little path so as to come up to the other side of the convent. They have to go up an exceedingly steep slope, and sit down to gather strength for the climb at the door of an old papermill, in the shade of an ancient walnut tree. A few feet away a most picturesque beggar is sitting in the sun picking lice. As soon as he sees the three men he gets up and comes over to ask for alms. He has on a beret which over the years has taken on the form of a cap, and wears his pants and jacket directly over his tough weatherbeaten skin. With his jacket open and his chest bare, Uncle Whirlwind looks like an old warrior in defeat, a routed captain who believes in nothing, hopes for nothing and fears nothing, not even the cold. He is dirty and unshaven but his face still shows traces of a kind of noble and sceptical artfulness. Uncle Whirlwind is an old-fashioned beggar who has a sense of pride about his profession, who knows his rôle to perfection; he never took things seriously, never worked, and has never had a sour attitude toward life.

One climbs up to the convent of Carmen by the slope which also leads to the hermitage of San Pedro de Alcántara; the grotto of St. John of the Cross is somewhat below it, and to the right is the hermitage of St. Theresa, standing out like the prow of a ship. All these places are extremely literary and are adorned with human bones and with clocks representing the life of the soul, with inscriptions alluding to the brevity of our hours and to that hour which awaits us all. To tell the truth, a visit to these places would not have an exactly therapeutic effect on an apprehensive or nervous person. St. John's grotto is half-ruined and its mouth is almost covered with weeds; to put it back the way it was when the saint used it would only be a matter of setting in a couple of beams, and the weeds could be burned out in half an hour.

The convent is only a hundred paces, perhaps less, from the hermitage. Nowadays it belongs to the Franciscans. A healthy-looking, redcheeked friar who smokes cheap cigarettes accompanies the traveler and his friends.

The traveler, who has a bit of family history related to the Order, talks with the friar.

"I had a great-uncle or great-great-uncle who was a Franciscan; he was martyred by the infidel in Damascus. He's been beatified, has been for a good many years now."

"What was his name?"

"Brother Juan Jacobo Fernández."

"I don't seem to recall him."

The friar didn't seem much interested in the Blessed uncle of the traveler.

"We're about to put new tiles on the roof and by next year, God willing, we intend to repair the gallery a little."

The friar, the traveler, and his friends go through the monastery and reach the library.

"We have four or five incunabula here; we've had them bound so that they won't fall apart."

The friar shows the traveler the incunabula with the pages chopped off, an inch on either side, by the binder's guillotine.

"We have a Museum of Natural History too, you'll see it in a minute. It's in very bad shape; when the Reds were here they made a terrible mess of it."

Seven years have gone by since the end of the Civil War.

The little procession goes into a classroom on its way to the Museum of Natural History. The boys stand up. It is curious to observe them; they are of all shades of hair, all kinds of faces and all ages.

"Most of the animals we have here are from the Philippine Islands."

The museum is all jumbled and covered with dust. It's a shame, but a shame which could probably be eliminated in a month if someone who knew his job would put things back in their places, aided by a maid with a broom in her hand.

The friar speaks of the misfortunes of the convent with a certain amount of indifference; it is as if he failed to realize that they were misfortunes, and what is worse, misfortunes that could be remedied so easily.

The convent is beautiful and full of tradition, and it occurs to the traveler to think what a pity it is that, like Pastrana, the convent seems incapable of doing anything for itself.

In Don Eustoquio's book, which is written in beautiful, flawless prose, he intones a lament to lost glories and sings the praises of past times, the times that for Don Eustoquio were best, no matter which they were. "Pastrana is today a ruined city. Yes, no longer do the doors of the fortress creak on their hinges, that fortress which in other times guarded the watches of the night; no longer does the martial air of well-equipped soldiers arouse in stirring hymn the warrior spirit of the medieval period."

The traveler believes that Don Eustoquio exaggerates. With neither night watch nor martial airs nor warrior spirit nor Middle Ages, Pastrana is a city like any other city (though beautiful as few are), which rises and falls, develops or becomes impoverished, depending on whether the Fates favor her or turn their backs on her. Perhaps there is to be found in Pastrana the key to something which happens in Spain more frequently than is necessary. Past splendor overwhelms and in the end exhausts the people's will; and without force of will, as can be seen in so many cases, by being exclusively occupied with the contemplation of the glories of the past, they leave current problems unsolved. When the belly is empty and the mind filled with golden memories, the golden memories continually retreat and at last, though no one goes so far as to admit it, there is even doubt whether they ever existed and there is nothing left of them but a benevolent and useless cultural residue.

Some say that Velázquez's canvas of "The Weavers" represents a weaver's shop in Pastrana. It is very likely that this is the case, but the traveler thinks that it would have been better for Pastrana to preserve the weaver's shop than a picture of it, however extraordinary, which, to cap the climax, is not in Pastrana either.

On the hill called La Cuesta de Valdeanguix, opposite the convent, are the long deep caves of El Moro, some of them as much as sixty meters in depth. The traveler neither climbs the hill nor enters the caves. Pastrana is a pretty big town to walk all over in one day, and the traveler feels he hasn't the strength to take another step.

Back in the inn on the plaza, he spreads out the map on the dining room table, as huge as a council table, and sets himself to thinking. To the south, in a bend of the Tajo, is Zorita de los Canes, that Alvar Fáñez* commanded.

Don Mónico has gone out and Don Paco is standing on the balcony looking off toward the valley. The traveler gets up, takes a little swallow of brandy, lights a cigarette, and goes to the balcony too; he gazes out over the plaza, above which an invisible, slightly languid breeze is idling. He looks toward the right, at the façade of the palace, which is in line with that of the inn, and sees almost within reach of his hand the grille which guarded the Princess of Eboli. The traveler, who is as much a Spaniard as any native of Pastrana, shudders when he thinks of the woman who dragged out her days and died at last

*Alvar Fáñez—lieutenant and trusted friend of El Cid (1040?–1099), Spanish warrior and hero. [Translator's note.]

on the other side of the wall; that enigmatic, beautiful, one-eyed lady, rather a bitch probably, who had so much influence and who drove frantic so many of the powerful. In Pastrana people call her crudely "the whore"; the Castilians are attached to their institutions and to the sacraments, and there are two things they will not give up for anything in the world: condemning the rich for flouting the Ten Commandments, and taking delight in always calling a spade a spade with the utmost cruelty.

"Well, did you like the town?"

"Very much. Pastrana is a fine city, a little sleepy perhaps."

Don Paco smiles thoughtfully. He says nothing for a little while, and then he turns to the traveler.

"We still have three hours of daylight. Would you like me to take the car out and drive over to Zorita?"

"I should say I would like it!"

The trip to Zorita is short and exceedingly pleasant. It seems odd to the traveler to travel so easily and rapidly. He had been used to measuring distances on the map by the number of walking hours, and by that standard he would have used up a whole day walking along the banks of the Arlés, as far as the place where it joins the Tajo, without encountering a single town.

Zorita de los Canes is located in a curve of the Tajo beside the useless supports of a bridge that never got built, surrounded by fields of hemp and lying at the foot of the ruins of the castle of the Order of Calatrava. All that is left of the castle is a bit of wall, two or three arches, and a couple of vaults. It is strategically placed on top of a small rocky hill which would be difficult to scale. On the hinder slope of the hill two little goatherds are tending a flock of goats; one of them is sitting on a rock whittling a crook out of ash, while the other is trying to coax a few tweets out of a reed flute.

The castle must have been a real fortress. Nowadays the arches and vaults look as if they were out of plumb, and threaten to tumble down from one day to the next.

The people in Zorita are agreeable and intelligent. According to what Don Paco tells the traveler, Zorita is a town where vaccination is no problem; you tell them they're going to be vaccinated, you talk to them about the advantages of doing so and the dangers of neglecting it, you set a date and when the time comes the whole town shows up *en masse*. All you need is one doctor and an orderly and the whole town is vaccinated in a single day. That's the way to do things!

The natives of Zorita de los Canes are of blond stock, like the Germans or the English. They have fair hair and blue eyes and are tall and well-proportioned. The girls comb their hair with a part in the middle and two braids; they all look very clean and shiny and the rosy color of their cheeks stands out on the white skin.

Zorita is a town where the people live, as it were, in one family, in peace and in the grace of God.

Across from Zorita on the other side of the river are the remains of the Visigothic city of Recópolis; and in the opposite direction, on the highway that goes to Albalata, one can just see Almonacid de Zorita, the town where the poet León Felipe worked as a pharmacist some quarter of a century ago.

Don Paco and the traveler depart from Zorita almost at nightfall; they have had something to eat in a tavern where the owners refused to charge for anything but the wine—because the rest was just what they happened to have on hand—and they have enjoyed themselves talking to the people.

During the return trip the traveler, sitting beside Don Paco, is thinking that his journey to the Alcarria is over. This idea makes him feel happy on the one hand and sad on the other. He has learned many things, and undoubtedly there are a great many more still to be learned. He walked where he pleased and when he didn't please he turned aside . . .

The jolting of the car makes him sleepy. His head nods a couple of times and he lays it on the shoulder of Don Paco the doctor, the man whose smile is always faintly, imperceptibly, remotely sad.

When they reach the Plaza de la Hora the traveler wakes up.

"Have you had a little nap?"

"Yes indeed; excuse me for leaning on your shoulder."

In the plaza the men are chatting in groups and the girls are walking up and down, surrounded by civil guardsmen in fatigue caps, young guardsmen who pay them compliments and turn their heads. Some little boys are playing leapfrog in one corner and in the opposite corner some little girls are playing hopscotch. An occasional young blade in a necktie crosses the plaza, and a graceful, pretty girl in elegant high-heeled shoes is laughing.

Night falls on Pastrana from the hill of El Calvario. The electric lights begin to go on and the loudspeaker of a bar flings a boogie-woogie rhythm against the ancient stones.

Don Mónico, Don Paco, and the traveler go into the club to have a vermouth and some olives stuffed with anchovies . . .

For further information about Granta Books and a full list of titles, please write to us at

Granta Books

2/3 HANOVER YARD

NOEL ROAD

LONDON

N1 8BE

enclosing a stamped, addressed envelope

You can visit our website at

http://www.granta.com